NORBERT GLAS was born in Austria in 1897. After receiving his medical degree at the Faculty of Medicine in Vienna, he practised medicine in Austria and later in England. He wrote numerous books that have been published in several languages. He died in 1986.

D1446565

READING THE FACE

Understanding a person's character through physiognomy

A spiritual-scientific study

NORBERT GLAS

TEMPLE LODGE

Translated from German by Pauline Wehrle

Temple Lodge Publishing
Hillside House, The Square
Forest Row, RH18 5ES

www.templelodge.com

Published by Temple Lodge 2008

Originally published in German under the title *Das Antlitz offenbart den Menschen* by Arbeitsgemeinschaft anthroposophischer Ärtze, Stuttgart, in 1961

A catalogue record for this book is available from the British Library

ISBN 978 1902636 93 1

Cover by Andrew Morgan Design
Typeset by DP Photosetting, Neath, West Glamorgan
Printed and bound by Cromwell Press Limited, Trowbridge, Wiltshire

Contents

Preface

When the author was a secondary school pupil it took him about 20 minutes every day to get to school by tram. He had to do this journey at least twice a day, often four times. Sometimes the boy did not feel like reading during the journey, or preparing for his lessons either. He began to prefer observing the faces of the people sitting or standing on his left or right. 'What do these eyes, noses, mouths signify?' he asked himself. They were all different. He attempted some kind of explanation for each part of the face; but he could not explain the form of the ears at all. And he started to observe the auricles of the people around him; a study which lasted for months, even years. He never grew tired of it, and went on to discover thousands of variations. But he could find no key to the problem, no real idea that would have divulged the secret of the form, the archetypal form.

Later on the young man became acquainted with Rudolf Steiner's anthroposophy. This brought him solutions to many of the riddles of existence both concerning the spiritual origin of man and also concerning the earthly phenomena of daily life. But the essential thing was to ask in a proper way, which meant to pursue the riddles wholeheartedly. And then one day it seemed as though a solution to the secrets of the human face was just asking to be found. After this, the kind of work gradually began that was to lead to a new physiognomy, which was only made possible by spiritual science.

One evening, on the occasion of a gathering of many doctor friends (presided over by Dr Ita Wegman whom Rudolf Steiner had elected to be the leader of the Medical Section at the Goetheanum) a question stirred the author into pouring his heart out. With the aid of a piece of chalk he endeavoured for the first time to explain to other doctors the form of the ear. In the excitement the sketches were drawn on doorposts. This particular evening became the starting point for the physiognomical essays in a periodical of that time, *Natura*. Again several years passed during which the first essays were altered, extended and supplemented. The draughtswoman, Miss Hanna Müller-Fürer, supplied any absolutely indispensable drawings.

One day the following happened. (This is being included here solely because a connection of destiny could well be of interest to some of the readers.) The manuscript was finished, all the pictures had been carefully stuck in, and the author took the package to Vienna where he had not lived for several years. He again went by tram (on the same line he had used earlier, on his way to school). He dismounted at a crossroads and ran directly into the arms of a gentleman who was no other than the owner of the publishing company Weidmann & Co. The gentleman was delighted about their meeting, as he had known the author when he was a little boy, and had not seen him for a long time. Because of this wholly unexpected meeting the manuscript found its way into the publishing company for New Medicine and was published in book form in 1935. Shortly before the annexation of Austria a new edition of the book was being prepared. But in the ensuing chaos the publisher lost his life, the publishing house was disbanded and the book remained out of print.

But over the many passing years the author has not only not lost his love for the forms of the human face but has today possibly an even greater interest in them than before. Many of the ideas have matured and gone through a change. And so, once again, in what is now the third edition, physiognomy is being presented to the public.

Introduction

Looking at the face of an adult it is immediately obvious that it is built up in three stages: the forehead section, reaching to the hairline, and the temples on each side; in the centre the nose with the adjoining cheeks dominated by the two eyes; and below this the lips which form the mouth, the chin and the lower jaw reaching out to the sides and upwards again.

These three areas are an image of the whole of the human being, and here Rudolf Steiner was the first to point in a fully conscious manner to its threefold nature both from the physical and the psychological point of view.

The head as a whole represents the 'nerves and sense system'. This is where most of the sense organs are concentrated. In addition, the nervous system shows its nature most strongly of all in the form of the brain, also where its weight is concerned. Perception, the having of mental imagery and thinking are activities of the life of the soul that are principally dependent on the processes in the nervous system and brain. The upper part of the head with the forehead and its surrounding area, the whole bony brain cover, could be taken to be a picture of the 'head' part of the head, that is, of the nerves and sense system.

★

The central organs localized in the chest, heart and lungs, are characterized particularly by rhythm; they represent the main part of the rhythmical processes in the human being, even though we can notice a rhythm taking place in many other parts of the body, the rhythm of the blood reaching even as far as the extreme periphery of the body. Also the activity of the kidneys and intestines take their rhythmic course. In fact our entire life comes under the effect of the rhythm of day and night, the changing seasons and the different periods of the paths of the stars, which influence us constantly, even if people are less aware of the latter than for instance the annual rhythm of summer and winter.

This portion of the human being, situated mainly in the structures of the central organization, Rudolf Steiner called the 'rhythmic system'. From the soul aspect this forms the foundation for our feeling. The most delicate interaction is to be found between the life of feeling and the heartbeat or the inhalation and exhalation of our lungs. In this connection it is especially important to observe what is happening in the soul, in particular, in the moment between two heartbeats or two breaths. One can well imagine that just at the very moment when nothing appears to be happening, during this lull of both pulse and breathing a soul process occurs.

This kind of conception of feeling being linked to the functioning of the heart and lungs does not sound quite so astonishing nowadays as it did at that time, when the idea of the threefold nature of the human organism was first expressed.[1]

Every layman today knows that having agonizing worries or neglecting the feeling life in the hustle and bustle of daily life can both make the heart ill and lead to ulcers. The heart is simply not being correctly nourished any longer, often even down to the physical level, as is shown in the degeneration of the heart vessels. The origin of the illness lies however in the feeling life, which no longer knows how to make proper use of its instrument, namely, the beating heart. And to the same extent as feelings become cramped and cold, the heart gets cramp too, whilst its special task should be to see that the right level of warmth is maintained.

Through the rhythm of inhalation and exhalation the soul element enters either more strongly or more weakly into the body. We know now as a matter of course that there are some forms of asthma where there is such strong bodily agitation that the patient can no longer breathe out normally, and therefore gets an attack of asthma. The breathing rhythm is then disturbed and the suffering this triggers is purely on the soul level. There is hardly a doctor who doubts this today. Such a disturbance is obviously also possible the other way round: for example, pollen or a process of poisoning in the person's own body can cause asthma. So the soul condition can be influenced by the bodily state. But what is important for our consideration, however, is solely the fact that the rhythm in these organs becomes as it were the instrument for human feeling life.

Just as the chest, the middle part of the body is the seat of the rhythmic organs and, in the soul province, of feeling, in this middle part of the face, feeling makes an image of itself in the form of the nose and the cheeks. This is where the mirror of the 'rhythmic system' is.

★

Beneath the diaphragm are the organs that have to do predominantly with metabolism. These are the stomach, intestines, liver, pancreas and everything belonging to them. Down here is really the centre of the metabolism, even though further up in the body there are of course very important smaller glands, whose functioning is absolutely necessary for bringing about rebuilding and construction within the human body. The work of the metabolic organs does not only enable life to be maintained, but also enables a force in the soul to resolve to *do* something. This 'metabolic system' is also the basis of the person's will-power. Unless the liver or the pancreas or the stomach are functioning correctly, what is received as nourishment cannot be digested. But the will, too, needs these organs as a foundation upon which to be active. If, for instance, the stomach is overloaded, people feel far less inclined to do some work. If the pancreas functions badly and the body no longer retains sugar adequately, and has to keep on ejecting it through the urine, then these people feel weak, particularly in their will, too; it will often occur to us, the will of these people has been weakened to such an extent that they are very open to being influenced by others. They fall in with outside advice far more readily than healthy people would do. Here is an example. Through an excess of alcohol a drinker eventually ruins his liver. His wife and his whole family make him promise to give up drinking, which he does with determination. But when a few days later a fellow drinker meets him outside the pub, he has to follow him in, despite his good intentions. Why? Because he has a liver that is ill and can offer him no support for his decisions; so he follows outside influence. His weakness of will has its organic basis in his liver, which has been ruined by alcohol. What has been described here in an extreme case applies to our whole metabolism. It has an influence all the time on our soul's will impulses. When people suffer from constipation, they are readily disposed to depression, which makes it very difficult for them to make decisions; they cannot make up their minds or they take longer to do so than someone whose intestines work less sluggishly.

There can be no doubt about it that there is a deep connection between metabolism and a person's actions. Whilst these internal organs are the important basis for the will, we need further organs that are actually in a position to carry out, outside, the will's intentions. The instruments for this are our limbs, for only with their help can we carry out our resolves. (This is the least that is needed if a person is healthy). Our legs and arms are influenced directly by the metabolism, just as their activation also works back strongly on the inner organs. (The nerve system enables this occurrence to come to our con-sciousness.) The reciprocal relationship between the activity of the arms and legs and the functions of the metabolic organs leads us to regard these two aspects as belonging together, both from the point of view of bodily processes as well as soul processes. Therefore Rudolf Steiner speaks of the 'metabolic-limb system' as the third part of our organism. It is the foundation and the instrument of our will. It finds its reflection in the lower third of the human face, i.e., in the region of the lips and jaw, which form the frame for the mouth. The nourishment that is taken in either in solid or liquid form and is passed on to the metabolism makes its way through this point of entry.

Chapter 1

SOME GENERAL ASPECTS
OF PHYSIOGNOMY

The new kind of physiognomy we are endeavouring to present here is based on the idea of the human being consisting of three parts, as was briefly summarized in the preceding introduction, and a few general facts of special importance will be covered here.

Let us begin by pointing out what needs to be known about the relative size of the three parts of the face. This already presents us with a few questions that have to be answered first, namely: when does the face stop growing?

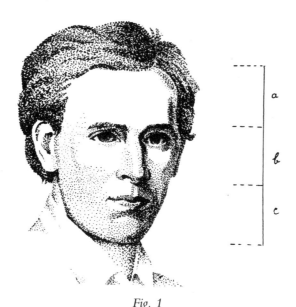

Fig. 1

This happens several years after puberty, around the twentieth year. From this time on, right into old age, the proportions remain more or less unchanged. Certain deviations will, however, receive some mention as we proceed. Ideally, lengthwise the three sections—the forehead, nose and mouth—are roughly the same size (see Fig. 1). If this is so it indicates a harmony between the three systems of organs and furthermore to a harmony between the three soul functions of thinking, feeling and willing, at least to a potential harmony. Looking at a face from the front we will measure it down the middle: from the hairline to the root of the nose (head system; Fig. 1, a), from the root of the nose to the transition from the nose partition to the upper lip (rhythmic area; Fig. 1, b), and from the beginning of the skin of the upper lip to the deepest point of the chin (metabolic–limb system, Fig. 1, c).

An excessive elaboration of one of these parts has its special significance, which is easily explained from what has already been said: increased development of the upper third compared with the other two sections points of course to a strongly formed head system or to a person who is particularly open to the upper forces working in forming the nervous system (Fig. 2, a).

Fig. 2

There are also people whose faces show to a very pronounced degree all the qualities that have to do with the middle section of their organism. Their noses are particularly conspicuous and point to an over-development of the rhythmic system. How this is to be evaluated will be left to a further chapter. To begin with we are looking at the general impression, a powerful development of the nose area, which leads us to ask what this directly expresses. Particularly characteristic are the protruding noses of musicians, artists or priests (Fig. 3, b, where the important thing is to what extent their noses stick out of their face).

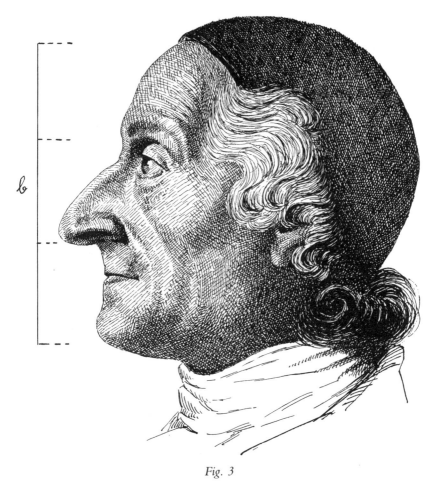

Fig. 3

Finally, some people have a pronounced lower half of the face, the mouth and chin section, which exceeds the size of either of the other parts. We could call them metabolic-limb types. Their will is usually the strongest component of their character, though for the present no explanation will be given to suggest in which direction their will is going. It is in their nature to be full of the urge to be active, to be driven, to assert their will.

The sort of personality possessing such strongly developed will may be an inspired general, a superb organizer, a boxer or even a skilled butcher (Fig. 4, c).

Fig. 4

★

Everyone has a facial form of their own. This sounds in the first instance like a platitude. And yet it is essential to emphasize this, because this phenomenon brings us to ask why this is so. The heads of lions, elephants, hares, canaries or lizards can only to a small extent be distinguished one from the other within their own species. In the case of human beings we can tell the difference between people because in the course of their lives their heads and faces are worked through by their individuality. Although animals also have souls, they lack an ego, for an animal body could never give expression to an ego. It takes years before a human organism is mastered and interpenetrated by its ego. This path of development is clearly mirrored in the face according to the threefolding. At birth healthy infants are relatively indistinguishable one from another. At the beginning the most characteristic part of each one of them is the forehead and the rest of the head, and somewhat later the eyes (we shall wait until later to speak about the ears). The skull is embryologically also the oldest part of them together with the central nervous system belonging to it. The embryo grows from the head downwards, and therefore the forehead part of a child's face is the earliest and most developed part of the child's whole form. The over-development of the upper half of the face is seen clearly in all the early pictures of babies (Fig. 5). This is a sign of the fact that the child's spirit makes its first entry into the body by way of the nerve-sense system. To start with, a child is predominantly active in its nerve-sense organism. The final form of the forehead is already being prepared in the second year, once the so-called fontanel (the skinlike covering existing at birth, the still divided halves of the frontal bone

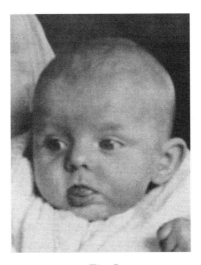

Fig. 5

Fig. 6

and the two parietal bones) becomes bony and joins together. If we look at the forehead of a two-year-old (Fig. 6) and of a four-to-five-year-old, we can quite easily picture what the forehead will be like in 15 to 20 years from then. There will hardly be any further change in the principal form, apart of course from acquiring furrows. As far as the length of time taken for development is concerned, this is quite a different matter when we come to the middle part of the face, particularly the nose. As we can see from the pictures of children (Figs 5 and 6), at the beginning of life very little development has occurred with regard to the nose. In fact it takes much longer for the personality to penetrate the rhythmic organism. If we take very careful note of how children's faces change over the years we notice that a transformation can be seen between their ninth and tenth year. Anyone familiar with Rudolf Steiner education knows that this period of a child's life is very dramatic. It can lead to a crisis which seems particularly to involve the life of feeling.[2] It is sufficient at present just to mention this increased sensitivity in the realm of feeling, as this is of course related to the entry of the human individuality into the rhythmic organism. During this period the nose begins to take on form more strongly, and in place of its more button-like shape it acquires a characteristic expression (Fig. 7). This crisis concludes with adolescence. During these assaults on the feelings or immediately in their wake the nose and surrounding area usually acquire the form that they keep for life, though it sometimes happens that after the middle of life

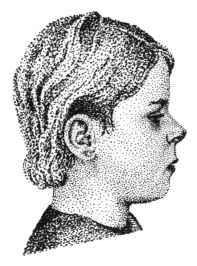

Fig. 7

and especially towards old age the nose can pass through further changes in its appearance. However, the form is basically complete around puberty or a little while afterwards (Fig. 8).

The lower part of the face takes the longest time to develop. There is no other area where small children look so similar to one another than they do in the area around the mouth. Their chin and lips are capable of change for a long time. The period around the twentieth year tends to be the time when the mouth begins to become really expressive. The mouth area continues to change as long as the person's

Fig. 8

ego is continuing to learn to liberate the will. Not until the middle of life, i.e., towards the thirty-fifth year and for a short time after that, does the lower third of the face reach the climax of its development. The modelling of the mouth is almost never concluded. Major changes also take place again in old age, but these can largely be attributed to a process of regressive development (Fig. 127, p. 133).

★

In every individual person a great many things are repeated, even if somewhat altered, which correspond to the entire history of humankind. In earlier times, for instance in the Egyptian era, the threefolding, which was described earlier, especially the threefold nature of soul experience, did nor occur to the extent it did later. This is why we see again and again in ancient Egyptian presentations portrayals of faces the form of which was far more integrated as a whole. The forehead and the nose often run into one another. In profile the nose appears far flatter and gradually disappears into the cheeks. In a downward direction the lips and the chin readily become part of the flowing line that begins above at the forehead. Because of the fact that ancient Egyptians bonded fully with the outer world— fused with it through both eyes and ears—adults also were to a certain extent like present-day children. The kind of life the ancient Egyptians led was lived predominantly in their sense organs. What they experienced was combined very intensively into a unity of perception, feeling and will. There can be no question of their possessing thinking in the present sense of the word. What comes to us through tradition shows us that in those times people were evidently entirely unable to arrive at thoughts independently. There was always a Godhead that looked down at them or to whom they bowed down when they experienced the power of the sun and the light. And they received this at the same time into their feelings and their will. Nowadays the thought of living our lives in this manner seems to posterity to be extraordinarily appealing, in the same way as observing small children can fill us with tremendous wonder. Physiognomically the evolutionary condition of humanity in Egyptian times came to expression in the relative uniformity of the shape of the face, and the division into three parts was not yet visibly defined (Fig. 9).

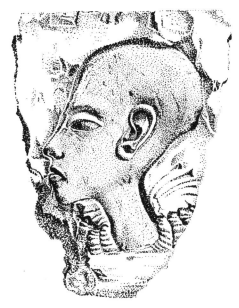

Fig. 9

This changed in the Greek era. Philosophy, real thinking, was not born in the West until Greek times. Yet among the Greeks this thinking did not only concern the head—even though Athene, thought-filled wisdom, arose in complete form from the head of Zeus. In Greek antiquity thoughts were still very much alive, arising in people's hearts, and just ascending from here into the brain. This was also how Aristotle conceived it, as Rudolf Steiner repeatedly described.[3] It is important and enlightening for physiognomy that where the Greek face is concerned we can speak of its twofold form, the nose reaching straight up into the forehead without a break, without the line being broken. Thought and feeling were partly fused into one. The mouth and chin, as the expression of the will, were on the other hand distinctly separate from the part of the face that is above it (Fig. 10).

After the Greek period of history, which Rudolf Steiner called the Graeco-Roman epoch, grouping them together into a larger historical unit, there followed the era to which we ourselves belong. The people of our epoch, especially from the fifteenth and sixteenth centuries onwards, and of course even earlier, show the clearly developed

Fig. 10

threefold form of the face. People are acquiring a greater and greater
aspiration to develop an individual will. Thinking acquires freedom,
which can become liberated from feeling, and the will struggles for
independence, to be free in its actions. Human beings' whole striving—and this is continuing very intensely right into our time—consists of the battle for the harmonizing of thinking, feeling and willing.
Whether the harmony is given in potential (Fig. 1) or whether one of
the three soul functions is particularly strongly or (weakly) developed
is manifested very clearly in the way the three parts of the human face
relate to one another (Figs. 2, 3 and 4).

Chapter 2

THE GENERAL PHYSIOGNOMY OF THE OUTER EAR

In the preceding pages we showed that the threefold nature of the human organism and the soul activities of thinking, feeling and willing bound up with this can be rediscovered in the three levels of the face. Each part of the face goes through a transformation in the course of life. Only the forehead attains its final form early on; the middle portion of the face changes more thoroughly and the development of the chin, lips and mouth requires the most time of all. Now there is, however, an organ in the head region which, although it grows larger after birth, no longer goes through any significant change of form; and this is the ear. Purely from the artistic point of view the two auricles round off the shape of the face. They have a relatively background position, as though shyly withdrawing; in fact women's ears are more or less covered by their hair.

At birth, the shape of every child's outer ear is already fully developed, and it remains unchanged for the rest of the child's life.

Where does this unchangeable nature of the form come from? It is a very old part of the human being. It is like a superb symbol of its past, the past of each individual.

The person's spirit, which begins to prepare its earthly body at conception, brings along with it the destiny from a previous earth life. This destiny enters, in the process of reincarnation (to use this word in Rudolf Steiner's sense), into the body, with the help of which it will either carry on its tasks in the course of its new life—or possibly leave them unaccomplished. Everything that comes into existence and everything that occurs is inscribed into the person's being, and in the final resort forms the face and transforms it in the course of years.

Only the outer ear is hardly affected by change. It can be regarded as a picture of the past life. What people bring into their new life in the way of capacities acquired in their past is conveyed to us in the form of their ears. Therefore this does not tell us anything about the new achievements of this life, or how people have changed in their inner being. Look at the way the school of life leaves its stamp on the way people look at you, and the expression of their lips! This does not apply to ears, because they are in fact memorials to the existence preceding this life. However, if we can read these ancient runes it will help us to see more clearly what gifts or weaknesses the person brings along at birth. And an education based on spiritual awareness will have to endeavour in the right way to overcome the weaknesses and cultivate the gifts.

★

The outer ear is not just the only important physiognomical part of the human organism that hardly changes from birth onwards, but it is also unique from another aspect, namely, in respect of its form it is a perfect image of threefold man. Also, from the point of view of size, the three areas are mirrored in proportion, just as this is also the case with the whole face.

Figure 11 is a demonstration of the three areas into which the ear can be subdivided. The upper part (Fig. 11, see '1') will, for the sake of simplicity, be called the head part. This has three parts (Fig. 11, a, b and

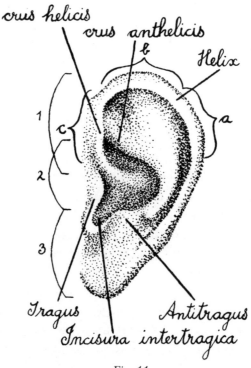

Fig. 11

c). It shows us the layout of the nerve-sense system and in the soul province the power of perception, the power of mental imagery and thinking.

The middle area, the expression of rhythmic man, forms a cavity that leads into the actual organ of hearing. Towards the back, the cavity is undifferentiated and remains round in form; towards the front, however, there is the so-called crus helicis, a projection in the form of a dynamic curve, dividing the cavity into two parts. The forces of breathing and blood circulation are mirrored in this middle part, and on the soul level it signifies the feeling life (Fig. 11, see '2').

The lower third symbolizes metabolism and has three parts, just as the top third has. They are formed out of a strong, button-like thickening (antitragus), an incision pointing downwards (incisura intertragica) and the soft, fleshy ear lobe. As the metabolic-limb system is the bearer of the will, the lower portion of the auricle reveals the strength and force of the will that one brings with one from birth (Fig. 11, see '3').

★

The position of the ears is normally on a level with the nose, from a little above the root of the nose to roughly the spot where the dividing skin in the nose runs into the upper lip (Fig. 12, b). The line where the ear begins in front (Fig. 12, B) is in very many cases almost parallel with a line one can draw from the topmost point of the forehead to the point of the nose (Fig. 12, A). However, the direction of the line is often determined by the course of the rear edge of the bone of the lower jaw. In any case the upper part of the ear normally lies further back than the lower part. The axle of the ear runs diagonally from behind on top to the front below. In most instances the ear lies in the same plane as the cheek (Fig. 12). It is important to be absolutely clear about the whole formation of the auricle. It will then be much easier to notice deviations. The differences are significant only when they appear really clearly; smaller fluctuations are found in a great many people.

To start with, it is of tremendous importance whether the ear is at the right height (i.e., roughly at the same height as the nose) (Fig. 12), or whether it has moved too far up (Fig. 13), or too far down (Fig. 14).

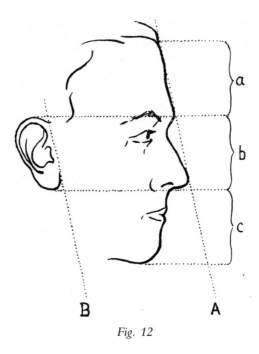

Fig. 12

This distinction, though, will not be so easy to see, where children are concerned, during the period before one is able to get a real idea of the relative size of the parts of the face, especially the nose. This cannot be finally judged until after puberty. An ear that is situated too low down usually indicates too strong a connection to the earth forces, the forces of gravity (Fig. 14). If, in contrast, you look at people whose ears

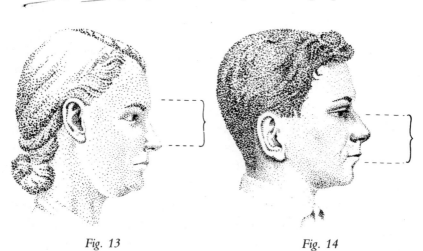

Fig. 13   *Fig. 14*

ears

are too high up, you will observe a number of things. But unless you really know the person concerned this cannot be completely interpreted. Generally speaking all you can say is that such a person has a certain reluctance to get involved in earthly matters. It does of course depend on the destiny of the individual person, in which direction this inclination will be expressed. She might perhaps produce fairly theoretical thoughts that are entirely intellectual and fantastic. This can go as far as actual fanaticism; but behind her ideas there is nothing real at all (Fig. 13). But there might also be people with this kind of ear who have a tendency purely from a physical point of view to have difficulty in moving their limbs properly; they can neither use their hands skilfully nor force their legs and feet to make a proper connection with the solid ground. Their real human spirit has not yet come fully to grips with the earthly realm.

Among the Greeks we often encounter the figure of the faun, a being that thinks up all sorts of tricks and plays fantastic, senseless pranks on people's instincts. The faun itself is distinctly egoless. When we see portrayals of it we are struck again and again by the way its ears are drawn upwards, and never show a harmonious construction (Fig. 15).[4]

Fig. 15

Another observation we can make is that some ears show a considerable divergence in their angle, which, as mentioned before, lies
diagonally from behind on top to below in front. It is comparatively
seldom that we see an ear with an exaggerated tilt at the top towards
the back (Fig. 16). People with this kind of auricle sometimes also
show signs of their inner state by having an elongated vertebral
column in the backward direction. This bodily position expresses a
certain overbearing attitude and exaggerated pride as well as a special
liking for keeping at a distance from their environment. It can also be
the expression of an insistent boasting about having a superior quantity
of intellectual knowledge. If this is very deeply rooted in a person's
nature then the two ears frequently have this over-strong tendency to
tilt backwards (Fig. 16). To a lesser extent this form can appear in a
person with too exuberant an imagination. If this tendency of the
upper organism is too overpowering for the metabolic system children
occasionally show a tendency to walk off with things they find lying
around them. They easily become kleptomaniacs, creatures with weak

Fig. 16

wills, allowing themselves to be led entirely by what they happen to see with their senses.[5]

This indication should suffice here, and is being included because there is still plenty of room for further study on the subject of the form of the ear being able to point to more deeply rooted kleptomania. As an example of this we are showing an illustration of the ears of a child with a very strong compulsion to steal, and whose auricle leans too far backwards. The child also has an active but superficial imagination that tends particularly in the direction of effusive chatter (Fig. 17).

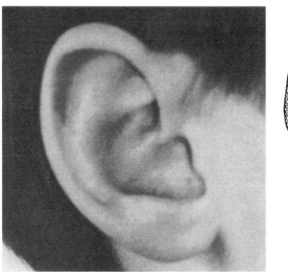
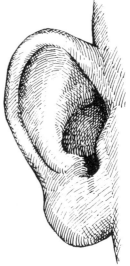

Fig. 17   *Fig. 18*

It is important to notice whether the ear as a whole is in the same plane as the cheeks, which is mostly the case, or whether the auricle sticks out to the side and, in most cases, more strongly towards the top. Ears that stick out show a weakness in making way for stimulating forces of form to flow into the body. This shows a lack of uprightness. This type of person finds it difficult to control their body, especially their limbs, with inner consciousness. Just as people who are tired and feeling weak collapse into themselves and sit there with their heads and shoulders hanging and their backs bent, ears that stick out and therefore lack firmness are a sign of weakness in people. It often happens that we shall find other symptoms of a lack of a formative force in children with this kind of characteristic. Among these are very large tonsils and adenoids, curvature of the spine and really flat feet. Now and then, if the ears stick out there is also evidence of a simplification of the inner structure of the ears. Everything appears less complicated in the dynamic structure, and this is repeated somehow, in a transferred sense, in people like this. They are, right from the beginning of life, more simple people. But this does not of course say anything about the way they may transform themselves in their inner being in the course of life (Fig. 18).

Ears that cling in an exaggerated way to the head are seen relatively less frequently. However, when they appear to a marked degree they indicate people possessing strong, possibly even over-strong form forces, who have too suppressed a nature and, when accidents happen, grind their teeth—though this tendency may have been overcome a long time before now, in the course of life's ups and downs.

And lastly, symmetrically shaped ears are among the diagnostic signs seen in general. Apart from small irregularities, most people have ears that both have the same shape, on the outside, and are at the same height. A clear dissimilarity is usually of considerable significance. The doctor and teacher should give special attention to a disturbance of symmetry, especially in the head area. Such deviations usually point to a weakness in the child's individual forces. We shall look into what the eyes can tell us when we come to the relevant chapter. Though not as often as occurs with eyes, there can actually be cases of 'squinting' ears, if it is permissible to use this expression in the case of the two auricles being different from one another. Whilst in ordinary life, as has been said, we only rarely see a striking dissimilarity, we often discover, when dealing with retarded children, different ear forms on the right from the left. In Rudolf Steiner's curative education attention is drawn again and again to the fact that in what we call retarded children the spiritual being cannot enter properly into the body, and therefore cannot work to develop it in a fully spiritually informed way. It is no wonder then that this shows in an especially invasive way in their ears, as these sum up so concisely an image of the personality (Figs 19a and 19b). The dissimilarity is usually seen in these children much more

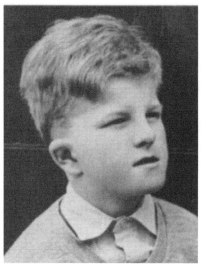

Fig. 19a   *Fig. 19b*

strongly in the upper third of their ears. For it is the upper forces that are primarily responsible for the creating of the form.

Here is an illustration of a boy who shows a particularly marked dissimilarity. Whilst the left ear, with regard to the angle, size and position does not seem to be badly formed (apart from the thickened top, the so-called helix), the right ear is strongly deformed (Fig. 20). It sticks out at the top. It also begins lower down. The top is thickened and flattened. We get the impression that a certain amount of weight is pressing down on it from above, causing the middle part to be reduced in height, so that it looks as though it has been squeezed. We can conclude from this picture that we have here a child whose ego is

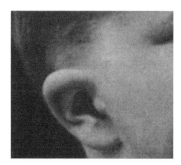

Fig. 20

going to have special difficulties in developing thought forces. These are subjected too severely to gravity. This keeps the feeling life restricted, which can only unfold with difficulty. There is also too much unformed substance in the lower part of the ear. A glance at the whole face of the boy confirms this impression. The lower jaw also weighs down much too heavily. Earthly gravity can obviously not be overcome from above. This can be observed quite clearly in the picture (Fig. 19 a, b), and will become even more comprehensible when we have gone into greater detail regarding the lower third of the face.

This should cover the most important of the general phenomena to do with people's ears. We shall proceed now to particular examples that are of special importance to us.

Chapter 3

PARTICULAR EXAMPLES OF THE PHYSIOGNOMY OF THE OUTER EAR

The upper third of the auricle, i.e., the so-called 'head part', gets its characteristic shape from the top ridge of the ear (helix) and the forward sweep of the inner side of the ridge (crus helicis). This breaks down into three different areas that clarify the picture. In the part that is turning in, a certain number of the organism's form forces are clearly mirrored (Fig. 11, a). The urge to harden and to form bones is seen here. If this is healthily formed, this ridge usually has a beautiful curve. Only towards the inside the rolled-in part remains somewhat open. This will also tell us the condition of the person's ability to hold themselves upright. The ability to stand upright and to walk depends in the first place on the bony system. If the bones become too soft, as is the case with rickets, for instance, this will delay the moment when a child learns to stand up or to walk. For in this case the bone-forming forces are particularly weak. A softening of this kind is not only clearly evident from the bones and the teeth, but over the whole of the organism, which also contains more water than a child who does not suffer from rickets. Without actually being ill, though, it can happen that people form organs that are too weak. At the same time it can often be noticed that the sense organs are less active. For instance, the eyes and ears are slow to react to stimulation, and can even be called sluggish. In a case as extreme as rickets, which is not seen very often these days but a few decades ago was very common, this slowing down was quite apparent. Children actually became inactive, on a mental level too, and took in outer impressions much more slowly. Even today we still encounter all these phenomena, but there is no need for the bones to be weak. It is not infrequently the case that these children, and adults too, tend to become obese, and are inclined to be of a phlegmatic temperament. The part of the ear that has to do with this is broader and softer than other people's. A glance at the small girl (Fig. 21) tells us straight away that this is a child who right from the start has the tendency to become fat. The part of her ear that we are talking about is clearly thicker (Fig. 22). As soon as this tendency is discovered in school, a proper education of the senses should be consciously set up. Attention should also be given to a suitable diet, i.e., the consumption of potatoes should be

Fig. 21

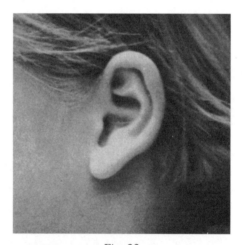

Fig. 22

reduced to a minimum; mealtimes should be in a regular rhythm, and no snacks between meals.

People who from birth onwards have more of a tendency towards a dissolving of form rather than a tightening up, will find time and again that in the course of their lives they are more exposed to inflammatory illnesses than other people. They will frequently suffer from colds of all kinds, which can lead to severe inflammations. This does not need to happen any more of course, as soon as they have succeeded in overcoming the weaknesses they brought with them at birth.

We see a totally opposite condition in people into whom hardening forces have penetrated too strongly. They develop in the course of life a certain rigidity in their skeleton, which brings on rheumatic ailments. The joints stiffen, and the spine loses a lot of its mobility. This hardening of the organism goes as far as the system of vessels, which likewise lose their elasticity. Arteriosclerosis builds up in the vessels. A person can have had a tendency to these symptoms right from birth. It leaves a certain impression on the ears. The area we were talking about becomes thin and the otherwise rounded furrow unrolls (Figs 23 and 24).

Nature sometimes gives us wonderful confirmation of things we already know. There is an illness—not all that frequent today—in

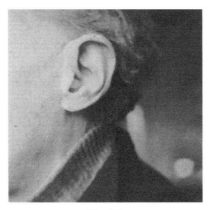

Fig. 23

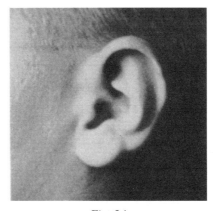

Fig. 24

which the organism deposits uric acid in certain places, and this is gout. The body is hardening to a mineral level in some areas. It is extremely remarkable for our considerations that a favourite place for this salt excretion is in the auricle, in fact in the upper third on the outside (Fig. 25). This of course is where we find a picture of the strong forces of form and of uprightness. (How the forces of uprightness play into this is seen in the fact that there is another characteristic place, too, where gout chooses to appear. This is the joint between the bone of the big toe and the adjacent bones of the middle foot. We use this joint very strongly when we walk. When the big toe has been hardened by gout, walking becomes very difficult. This over-mineralization, then, disturbs the uprightness to a certain extent. Such processes show us real connections between certain bodily forces and particular places in our physique.)

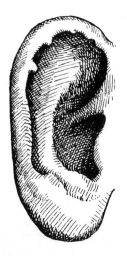

Fig. 25

★

The next section of the upper third of the auricle, which we will now consider, comprises the top part (Fig. 11, b). What we can call a well-developed example is one that has a beautiful shape which is almost a half-circle, and which in addition to this neither has a break in it nor sticks out (Fig. 26). For a perfect formation the helix has to roll in in a regular way. Its thickness should hardly alter at the different heights and maintain its proper relationship to the rest of the ear. The illustration shows us what is meant here. In this part, which we have to study in great depth to recognize either its beauty or its shortcomings, we see that what is being expressed is the ability that a person is born with to think. Both the powers of vivid mental imagery and the ability to form clear concepts are indicated in this section. Only it is hard to see from this part of the ear in which of these two directions future development will go. There is some certainty that the possibility exists here of an excellent all-round capacity to think, if the form is as harmonious and geometrically beautiful as in Fig. 27. Only we may perhaps be permitted to add that if in the direction of the neighbouring area to the back we notice more of a thinning of the helix and a tendency to unroll (i.e., in the direction of the section that has to do with the forces of form) then superficiality and unreality can occur in the thinking, and this indicates abstractness and shallowness (Fig. 28, over).

The basic form for sound thinking, however, can diverge in two directions, either of which can be mirrored symbolically in the ears. Clear thinking is dimmed in the case of people who let their ideas degenerate into fantasy or actual lies. If this quality is deep-seated, the top of the ear will lose its lovely even curve. It will tend towards

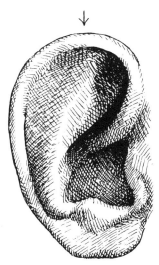

Fig. 26

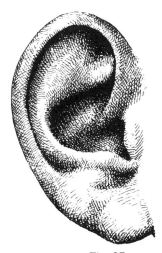

Fig. 27

becoming pointed. If this is seen in children it is serious enough to prompt us to re-enforce their teaching with lessons to encourage love of truth and respect for the reality of life. This sort of ear shape does not occur very often (Fig. 29).

On the other hand we encounter fairly frequently the other deviation, namely, the flattening of the top of the ear. Such ears almost always point to weak thinking forces (Fig. 30). Children will have considerable difficulty with learning; they lack intelligence right from the beginning.

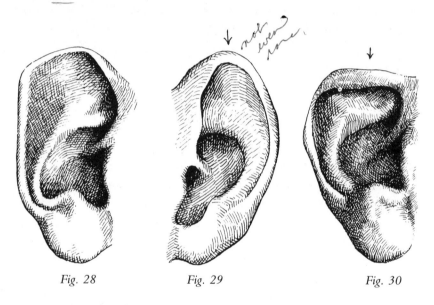

Fig. 28   *Fig. 29*   *Fig. 30*

So the second region of the upper ear conveys to us a picture of how much thinking power and the power of mental imagery a person has brought with them into life.

★

The third area in the upper third of the auricle comprises the rim that rolls into the ear from above (Fig. 11, c) and is part of the 'region of thought'. In this part we see an expression of the amount of drive a person has. Looked at from a more organic point of view, this region tells us something about what kind of strength people have in their speech. Some people form their speech easily; they can express whatever flows into their life of thought. The upper curve continues on into the front one with a kind of harmony, following the line of the circle that began above (Fig. 27). But other people may have a reserved nature that causes their speech to stream forth just as reluctantly, making them unable to express what lives within them.

In the first case, in the people gifted in speaking, we meet with a beautiful, sweeping form which is usually clearly defined (Fig. 31), whereas a break in the circular bend indicates a clumsy way of speaking (Fig. 32, over).

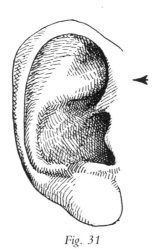

Fig. 31

The next formation shows particularly strikingly what is meant here (Fig. 33). The person to whom this ear belongs, and whose nature points to various artistic talents, suffers from a decided speech impediment. In his case the 'speech line' is drawn straight downwards. Hand in hand with this we find a certain lack of freedom in the soul realm. There is no doubt about there being something wrong with the speech ability of the person whose ear is being shown in Fig. 34. It belongs to a man who is deaf and dumb. What strikes us most of all is that here in front we see the helix going straight downwards. The picture may well speak for itself. But let us mention one thing: the spot we mentioned in regard to the ability to speak actually says nothing about the ability to hear.

If we now survey the three particular areas that are documented in the upper third of the ear something very remarkable comes to light. Both our capacity to be upright and our sense perception are shown in

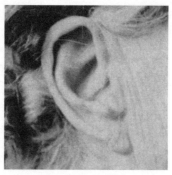

Fig. 32

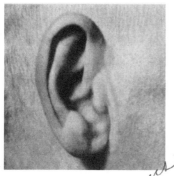

Fig. 33

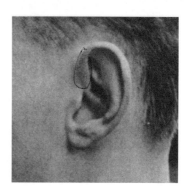

Fig. 34

the first section, the power of mental imagery and of thought in the second, and the power of speech in the third. In Rudolf Steiner's way of seeing things these are the three most important achievements of children up to their third year: standing upright, thinking and speaking. These, however, are the very abilities we human beings have through which we manifest our personality. By their means our ego comes to particular expression and stamps our individuality upon our bodily nature. When this process has come to a certain conclusion human beings can address themselves as I. This happens, as we all know, around the end of the third year.

★

Whilst the structure of the upper part of the auricle has more of a planelike/linear character and therefore its three different sections are to be recognized and distinguished more easily, it is much more difficult to present the middle section of the ear. The central third consists especially of two parts: the one, continuing on from the helix, is called the antihelix; the second is formed by the cavity which actually belongs to the entrance to the ear. These two structures are an image of the rhythmic organism and consist accordingly of two areas that, although belonging together very closely, are definitely distinguishable from one another: the breathing organism and the circulation system. The exterior antihelix, with its two upward-pointing sides, is the picture of the breathing organization.

The other part of the rhythmic areas consists chiefly of hollows and small cavities. These lie very close to the 'breathing' part of the ear; in a certain respect they appear like its negative, at least at the spot where they touch the respiration area. We can see from the whole structure of the ear (Fig. 11) how far the lower boundary reaches. This second section of the central auricle is the expression of the heart and circulation forces that people bring with them into this world.

★

Breathing and circulation belong very closely together and form the 'rhythmic system', yet they are not only easily distinguishable from the physiological point of view, of course, but also in the manner in which they form the foundation for soul processes. Feeling, with its many gradations, has as it were two main directions. One of them, being more supported by the breathing, strives upwards and joins with the part of the human being that manifests in speech and thinking. For example, the world of feeling makes its way into what we can express in speech; if this happens to an adequate extent our speaking comes to life and is ensouled by the breath stream. In addition, along with the breath and with the lively support of the circulation, of course, feeling carries forces into our active thinking, giving it the possibility of true understanding. A more sensitively tuned soul observation will easily recognize that 'understanding' is always accompanied by a gentle inflow of feeling, which is largely due to the breath and, to a certain extent, the rhythm of the blood as well. The kind of understanding that is meant here leads to a genuine, true power of 'reason'. This is different from what we call thinking in the ordinary way.

The other main direction feeling takes—and at present people have given this pride of place—points to the rhythm of the circulating blood. The heart becomes its sensitive organ, sending heartfelt warmth right into the will. In this way the world of feeling enters deeply into human action. We can become aware of this if human action is really carried by moral feeling—meant in the best sense. When people perform an unselfish action, for instance saving someone's life, we can easily see that it comes from the heart, is even an inspired action. But even less noble actions, happening perhaps from out of an unconscious urge, are accompanied by a feeling undertone supported by the pulsating blood. The collaboration of breathing and circulation in the middle organism and the reflection of both of them in the life of the soul gives us an understanding of why Rudolf Steiner called the part of the soul that lives predominantly in the feeling the 'rational or the perceptive soul'.[6]

These two components 'rationality' and 'perceptive warmth', despite forming a unity in the ear's physiognomy in that they both belong to the middle part of the organ, are nevertheless distinguishable in their twofold nature, however strongly they play into one another.

★

If we try to go deeply into the forms that have more to do with the breathing area of the middle ear—starting to do this to begin with the help of intuitive imagination (not of the fantastic kind!)—we shall notice the following: the curve that is gradually becoming narrower as it goes down leaves room for the 'cavity of the heart'. By comparison the 'breathing form' broadens more and more as it goes up. It is immensely interesting and impressive the way the two sides of the antihelix divide. One of them is striving upwards, clearly towards the top of the ear, disappearing into the region of 'thought'. The other, however, goes into the front bend of the crus helicis, coming to an end in the part that belongs to the picture of the speech faculty. Here we have a symbolic image of what we presented before in thought-form: the feeling that plays into the breath reaches on the one hand into the realm of human reason and on the other hand into the human activity of speaking. The heart's warmth pulsing in the blood is still being tenderly embraced by the breath of speech, although its important place is in the cavities of the heart which alternately draw in the blood and then release it, and which are depicted in the middle depressions of the ear and finally reach down towards the lower third of the auricle. The lower limit is indicated by way of a deep incision above the so-called antitragus, and this is almost always to be found. This becomes the back boundary, whilst the front one can be found roughly in the middle of the tragus. It strikes me as more than playing with pictures when the middle ear is described as mirroring the lungs and the heart. In the same manner as the lobes of the lungs surround the organ of circulation, the two sides of the antihelix partly encompass and surround the cavities of the ear.

★

We are able to judge how people are predisposed in their breathing by distinguishing exactly the course taken by the front and the upper ridge and their amalgamation in the antihelix. A ridge that descends with a good curve is bound to pull downwards with the kind of thrust that produces an even furrow between the helix and the antihelix (Fig. 35). This will form such a consistently curved line that it tells us that people who show this have good control of their whole breathing organism. In other words, this indicates that their soul nature has good mastery over the body. The ability is present for the personality to ensoul its thoughts. The opposite of this is depicted by a flattening of this area; this part can become very thin at the top, spread out too widely so that the furrows and cavities cannot come into their own.

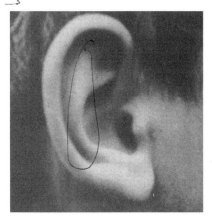

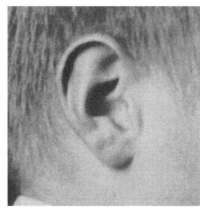

Fig. 35   Fig. 36

This often expresses a weakness of the life forces, when the freshness of thought is then similarly flattened. Thoughts become dry, abstract and papery, the quality of breathing life cannot get into them any more (Fig. 36). Some kind of speech disturbances often accompany breathing difficulties. In Fig. 34, the ear of a young person who is deaf and dumb clearly shows this. The front ridge of the antihelix, which belongs to the front bend of the helix, is very thin, a little bent, and also lies too close to the 'speech curve'. In fact in the case of most deaf and dumb people, especially when they try to talk, we can hear how uncontrolled their breath stream is. In cases of asthma, especially of course when it occurs early, existing since birth for example, we frequently find either that the lower front ridge is a bit stunted or that the crus antihelicis comes too close to the front curve of the crus helicis. In the particular case of the young man who is deaf and dumb there is the additional problem that he also suffers from hay fever and hay asthma. There is then a double reason for the breathing disturbance, which consequently creates such an interesting picture in the corresponding parts of the ear.

Nature creates wonderful examples, and does experiments, to reveal to us its powers! We have stressed how our speech activity and our breathing are connected; and yet the two are distinguishable. This is shown in the picture of a person (Fig. 33) who on the one hand has a defect in speaking and in his ability to express himself, but on the other hand has an outstanding breathing rhythm which enables him to be able to walk for hours without any difficulties. He was born with an outstanding rhythm in every regard, without which any musical activity is doomed. His ear clearly shows both a weakness in the speech area and a strong foundation in his breathing. It also points to an even stronger variation in the strength of the breathing, and we see this in the way the curve of the antihelix moves round towards the back. If the expansion is beautiful but not exaggerated such a form frequently gives evidence of a kind of courage, which is appropriate in the middle area.

Regarding the middle ear it is of great importance in coming to a judgement about its form to acquire an idea as to whether really strong formative forces were at work (as for instance in the previously mentioned Fig. 33 of a person gifted with outstanding rhythm), or whether all the forms in that region have more of a tendency to be indistinct, and even to the touch are soft and lacking in firmness.

★

To form a judgement with regard to the system of cavities in the middle part requires our going into important detail. An unbroken curve, covering about a third to a quarter of a circle, is a promising one. But at the same time it should have cavities that are sufficiently deep. If both these requirements are present (Fig. 33) this frequently points to a rich feeling life, which can also be indicative of a significant relationship to musical experience. Organically, such forms usually reveal a good circulation and a strong heart. It is obvious that the strength in people who are artistic is bound to be anchored in the middle part, just as all the emphasis falls on the rhythmic system. Divergences from this ideal form exist of course in every direction. Indentations towards the back appear particularly often. These are sometimes so strongly in evidence that the outer furrow, which already belongs to the antihelix, is pushed aside. Ears like this tell us that these are people who live very strongly in their feeling life, and are strongly engaged in their own feelings. Outwardly they can appear to be very reserved. They live more in themselves, like a snail that likes best of all to creep into its shell. They have difficult natures, yet they can make extraordinarily valuable contributions provided they can master the superabundant forces in their middle organism. They may also become very taciturn people with the appearance of being mysterious (Fig. 37).

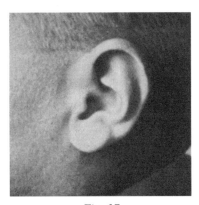

Fig. 37

Characteristics in excess of these appear in the form of pathological conditions. This can be the case when the feeling is directed more towards the metabolism and gets entangled there as it were. People can then possibly become prisoners of their lower organization, especially when this remains sluggish and weak (poor digestion and hardening are signs of this). Such people turn into pathological melancholics. This finally reaches the point of real melancholy, when the people suffering from this are forced in their life of feeling to participate so intensively in the sluggish behaviour of their intestines or liver that they do not want to do anything any more; they sink into themselves and all they can feel is earthly weight and its suffering. This can be expressed in a certain way in the ear (Fig. 38): the lower part of the curve in the middle area is exaggerated, and points more in a downward direction, as the illustration shows. It belonged to a patient who suffered for a long time with such intense melancholy that it called for a long stay in an institution.

A contrast to this is seen in the kind of changes appearing when the curve enclosing the cavities has either been shifted or bent, or the whole area is too small and much too flat. The ear of a child with special needs, whose trouble is located very strongly in its feeling life, is an example. In this case (Fig. 39) all that is retained of the circle is only about an eighth at the most, and at the other end of it there is, instead of a curve, a bit snapped off at an angle.

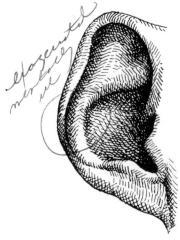

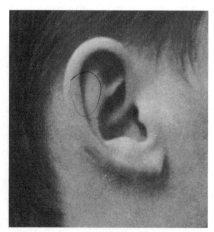

Fig. 38   Fig. 39

Very constricted, with little depth to the cavities, is the ear of a man (Figs 40 and 41) who for many years suffered from aortic stenosis. Here is a good illustration to show how the weakness in the circulation system seen in the case of an organic heart defect can be mirrored in the 'heart region' of the ear. In this case you can see at the same time that the breathing and the blood organization have to work closely together.

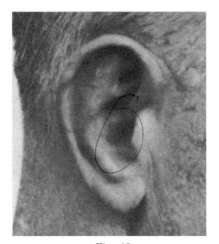 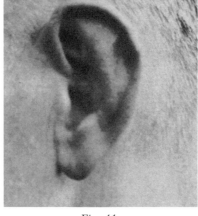

Fig. 40   *Fig. 41*

★

It seems relatively straightforward to sort out the different parts of the upper or middle ear. But to see clear divisions in the lower section proved very difficult for a long time. Eventually, though, one discovers obvious distinctions in the bottom third, too, and it can also be seen as a mirror of the situation in the metabolic–limb organization.

Where the individuality of a person is concerned it means a great deal if there is a clear division of the three systems, both from the points of view of the body as well as of the soul. A blurring or dissolving of boundaries can prove serious. Like two gatekeepers, to use an image, even if it strikes some people as too bizarre, there are two lumps of cartilage in front of the entrance into the underworld of the metabolism; these two guardians themselves belong to this third realm. We are talking about the tragus and the bit on the other side, the 'antitragus'. They present an image of the functioning of the lymph

and glandular system. We might be able, as well, to see from the way
these are formed how dynamic the person's fluid organization is. If this
is healthy, there should be a certain distance between these two points,
that is, they should not be either too far apart or too close together
(Fig. 42). A good example of a narrow construction is of the ear of a
retarded child who became much too fat, and whose tendency in this
direction has to be attributed to a glandular disturbance. The striking
narrowness of the lower break in the auricle (incisura intertragica)
(Fig. 43) is also partly due to the fact that the tragus and the antitragus
have come too close to one another. At the same time we shall often
encounter a thickening on the upper third of the ear on the outside
towards the back, that is, at the place where there is a particular
indication of the relation to the form-giving forces. People like this,
with a tendency to dispense with form and grow fat, will show a
phlegmatic temperament.

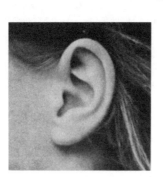

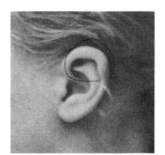

Fig. 42   Fig. 43

It is easy to find the opposite to this. This is when the tragus and the
antitragus are too far apart (Fig. 44). Here there is a predominance of
the risk of too much entering the glandular system and possibly
overwhelming the person. This occurs for example in people who
suffer from an overactive thyroid; they are excessively excited, their
whole metabolism goes too fast, and they readily lose weight and grow
very thin. They are often exaggeratedly sanguine in temperament, and
are ruled by the unconscious forces of their metabolism (Fig. 45). The
boy shown earlier on in Fig. 17 can also be taken as an example of this.
His ear is a clear example of the tragus and antitragus being far too far
apart. At present he shows no signs of anything wrong with his

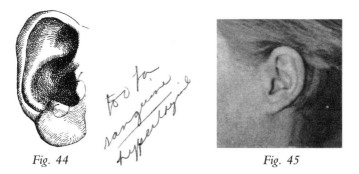

Fig. 44   *Fig. 45*

thyroid, but his whole character gives it away that he is driven by his instincts, the unconscious part of his being rising up out of his lower organism. His temperament shows a marked sanguinity; he is fairly imaginative and extremely talkative. His urge to go off with things that do not belong to him is a sign that he cannot control his unconscious (Fig. 17). As the form of his ears shows, there is no distinct division between his middle and his lower organism, which explains why he does things that are not under the control of his consciousness. A well-formed tragus and antitragus that are at a harmonious distance from one another can be observed in people who have great skill in their hands and fingers. And their character shows an immediate willingness to help others.

★

The next form to be distinguished in the lower ear is the gap dividing the tragus and the antitragus. This gap, its width, depth and shape, will of course always have a close connection to the two 'gatekeepers' to the lower region. This is obvious, because the individual functions of the metabolic system are very closely bound up together. However, the incisura intertragica is more a picture of the deeply buried processes in the organism; we have to think rather of the phenomena to do with the processes in the intestines and kidneys in so far as these are more linked to the transformation of substance than of the processes leading to the excretion of waste matter. The gap can form a beautifully harmonious line, which everybody will immediately recognize as such (Fig. 46); and going from this regular form there are all the other gradations in the direction of a form which gets wider and wider,

and which indicates a lively capacity for transformation in the metabolic system (Fig. 44); while a narrowing, as seen in the previously
mentioned child, draws attention to a decided weakness operating
even deeper within the organism than only in the field of the glands.
We mentioned this in particular before (Fig. 47).

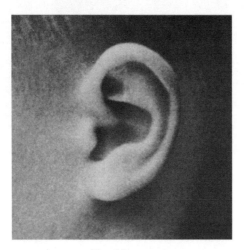
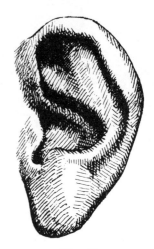

Fig. 46   *Fig. 47*

★

The third area in the lower third of the ear, which is also of special
importance, is the ear lobe. It is the living expression of the inner force
that builds up the human organism, its ability for constant regeneration; and the ability to reproduce also partly belongs here. There is
actually a mirroring here of the polar opposite forces to those that are
expressed in the back part of the upper ear (Fig. 11, a). That is where
we see the disposition of all the form forces to a hardening and also the
effective functioning of the senses. These forces of rigidity can, in the
case of illnesses such as gout, not only take hold of the upper body, but
become visible as hard little knots just in this particular place and stem
from little crystals consisting of salts of uric acid. Look at the ear lobe in
comparison. It is totally free of gristly substance, and is the softest part
of the outer ear. In our body the will is anchored predominantly in the
metabolic system, which creates its mirror image especially expres-
sively in the ear lobes. Ear lobes can be very different. Those that are
harmoniously rounded (Fig. 48) are roughly a third of the ear in size.

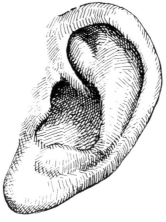

Fig. 48

We have also to mention the ear lobes that have a slight point at the bottom, and these give not so much a picture of the total will forces as a picture that emphasizes the force of sexual reproduction. The custom of wearing earrings has to do with this side of the metabolic organism; it is intended to increase awareness of the power of procreation (Fig. 49, over).

Broad, almost square ear lobes are a remarkable phenomenon, and their owners usually have strong metabolic systems; while their metabolic strength usually provides them with a good basis for a strong will. People who are typically choleric often show forms like this (Fig. 50).

It is of decisive importance to everybody what kind of will organization they have. Have they come down to earth showing that they want to work to the full extent of their capacities or will they have reservations regarding what they do? The kind of will-power they have is characterized right from the beginning of life, by which of these directions is typical of them. They will be more inclined to be active, to 'go for it', or they will prefer to let things take their course without their having to do anything about it. If we want to classify people in this way, we could also say: the one sort develop a strong will, which shows an urge to do things out of their own initiative, whilst the other sort seem to have been born with a weak will. The ear lobe is significant for showing this strength or weakness. In fact the

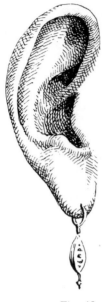

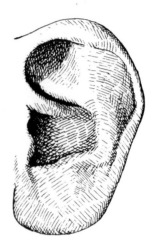

Fig. 49   Fig. 50

kind of ear lobe that has a loose bit hanging down shows the push to be free, the force of free will, whereas the ear lobe that is a continuous part of the ear is a sign of a weakly disposed will system. The best thing to do is to line up both kinds, the kind that hangs loose and the kind that has grown together with the rest of the ear, in one picture (Figs 51 and 52). People with loose-hanging ear lobes are personalities who are prepared to use their legs and feet to go forward with determination.

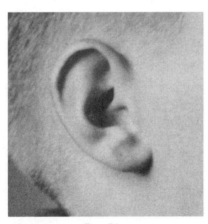
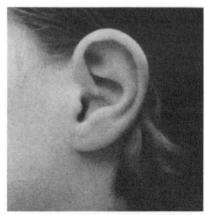

Fig. 51   Fig. 52

People who possess more the grown-together kind appear to find it far more difficult to use their limbs to move freely on the earth.

All that we have said in this connection has nothing to do with what an individual can work to achieve despite a tendency that was originally different. We have finally managed to find three different parts in the lower ear, too, which mirror the metabolic system:

1. The area of the tragus and antitragus as a picture of the lymph and glandular function, and also altogether as a token of the liveliness or weakness of the metabolism.
2. The area of the gap tells us something about the nature of the work going on in the intestines and kidney system in the transforming of substance.
3. The ear lobe, which becomes an image of the mobility of the processes in the lower organism and reminds us once more emphatically that the will has its basis in the metabolic-limb system.

★

In presenting the physiognomy of the outer ear we have succeeded in bringing real order into our considerations of this strange structure. It becomes a book in which we may read something about a person's history. But a past history is all we glean from it, disclosing to us nothing of the future even though, of course, we may deduce something from the past that tells us of a future course.

At the conclusion of these descriptions concerning ears I will endeavour, for those who take an interest in and enjoy finding out about further spiritual connections, to present the cosmological background that led to the formation of this organ.

Rudolf Steiner showed us in a great number of different descriptions in what ways the human being comes under the influence of cosmic forces. These have to do with stellar activity. It is important, for instance, to think of the spiritual influences that come from the planets. These concern primarily the seven planets already known to the ancients. Rudolf Steiner described these forces by way of his own research, and told us in what way stellar influences affect the human organism. I will run through this briefly from the point of view of our particular purpose. Those who have greater interest will find all this dealt with at length in the works of Rudolf Steiner. For now we will restrict ourselves to going through the list of what each planet does. First comes Saturn, the most distant of the seven, the planet that has to do with the forming of the bones, the sense organs, and the hardening process in the organism. Secondly, Jupiter has the primary task of forming the brain, the organ of thought formation. Thirdly, it is Mars that is occupied in the construction of the speech organs. These are the three planets that are positioned above the sun, and after these comes the sun realm, the forces of which work to form the breathing and circulation. Then in fifth place comes Mercury, which influences our glands and lymph system, in sixth place Venus, which influences the region of the kidneys, and in seventh place the moon, which is involved in the widest sense with the reproductive organs (these last-mentioned planets are also said to be the ones that are positioned below the sun).

This very rough enumeration, which could of course be taken much further and given in detail, will have to suffice. In fact we can quite clearly identify that ears simply do show a mirroring of all these planetary influences. Human beings are particularly subject to these influences during embryonic development. These influences are above all dependent on what kind of destiny we have formed for ourselves in an earlier life on earth. Whilst the effect of this on the rest of our organs is more in its potential possibilities, because our organism is of course far from finished at birth, the outer ear by the time of birth has already been given the full impress of its form. No further change can come about; a person keeps it, unchanged, for the rest of life; and this is quite understandable, because the past as such is unalterable, however much we can alter or fulfil our destiny in our new incarnation. So the outer ear is a picture of the way the planets influenced human beings in their previous incarnation. What they bring with them from that life in the way of abilities or the lack of these is written into the runes of the ear. So it is no wonder that it is so difficult to interpret this script. And anyone who has patiently followed all these explanations with good will may, by the end of them, easily ask: and why is it particularly the ear that shows us these things? To this, I would like to offer a modest supposition that can be arrived at out of Rudolf Steiner's wisdom. There was an occasion when he emphatically stated that the ear in particular had once been an all-embracing organ that had included the whole of the human being. In the course of a long development this organ went through a process of shrinking until it had become the ear we know today. The author believes it to be the case that the auricle still retains a last memory—what science today might call a rudiment—of that all-embracing organ. And each time we are reborn a seal of our past is stamped on us in this way.

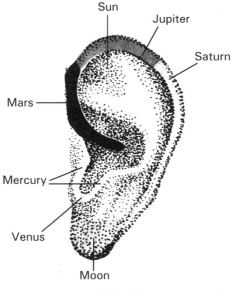

Fig. 53

So a certain constellation of the stars puts its seal on our ear, leaving with us at birth an image of our past. May this justify me when, as though summarizing this, I described the parts of the ear shown in the proceeding picture. This corresponds, like a kind of shorthand, to everything I endeavoured to explain in detail about each of the seven areas (Fig. 53).

Chapter 4

THE PHYSIOGNOMY OF THE FOREHEAD
AND THE HEAD

The physiognomy of the human forehead is inseparably connected with the form of the skull, the solid covering of the brain. Its shape is also essentially dependent on the formation of this central organ of the nervous system. Even though the forehead is our main consideration, for the sake of completeness we shall have to include a survey of the connection this has with the rest of the skull. To do this it is advisable to study the skull of a skeleton in a more artistic way. This means just to try to look at the dome of the head as though we were enquiring about the living forces that formed this dome. We shall do this to start with without drawing on the relevant explanation regarding brain development, which does of course, in the last analysis, concern the formation of the upper skull bones.

As we are looking here at solid substances, very similar to that of an architectural construction, the forces of direction in space obviously play an important part. If we investigate these forces we easily discover the presence of three directions in space (Figs 54 and 55). In front, at the forehead, a force is at work moving in an upward direction. It goes upwards from the level of the root of the nose creating the actual curve

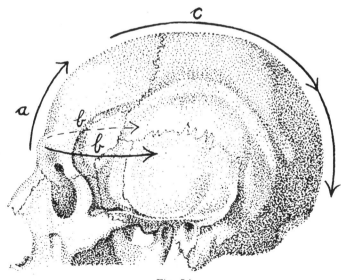

Fig. 54

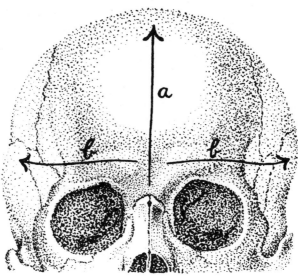

Fig. 55

of the forehead (Figs 54, a and 55, a). Above the eyes, forming forces move both to the right and to the left, to the temples (Figs 54, b and 55, b), and finally a third force moves from the top of the head, in a vigorous sweep downwards to the back of the head (Fig. 54, c).

The head, as far as it can be seen as the protective covering of the brain, expresses human thinking. As far as the forehead itself is concerned, this seems to be more or less the general rule. However, when we are speaking about the whole of the skull, we have of course to distinguish more exactly between the different areas we experience in our thinking. The form of the forehead shows above all the kind of thinking that takes place in pictures, mental images, concepts, and also indicates a person's ability for sense perception. All this is 'inscribed on a person's brow', though how we learn to read it we shall attempt to show in the following way.

Where thought, especially its development, is concerned, the elements of percept, mental image and concept are absolutely essential—but this can lead to problems if this thinking concerns us further, as human beings. We could ask for instance: which areas are also affected by the thought processes? For actually to a certain degree a further part of the soul besides thinking becomes involved when we engage in thought activity. Even if it remains more or less unconscious, a feeling usually creeps in, accompanying the thought process. This may possibly seem to be only like a shadowy dream, unlike our thought images, which are as clear as day. It is as though a feeling of enthusiasm or courage, fear, depression or longing were hovering in the background and might very rapidly rise up from the subconscious into consciousness.

If we are going to speak about the sensations that accompany thoughts we must be acutely alert as to what is meant by this. These are feelings appearing alongside thoughts and which can even colour them; yet we must nevertheless not try to blur them.

It is necessary to state this, to find our way to an understanding of the forming force accompanying our thinking processes. This feeling force that accompanies thinking and as it were resonates together with it comes to expression physiognomically in the area of the temples and the adjoining area of the top of the head. To anticipate any contradictions, let us remind ourselves that from the organic point of view the world of feeling is connected as closely as is possible with the rhythm of the blood and the breathing. To what extent, however, this is affected by our thought process and becomes mirrored as a matter of course up in the brain region can be identified in the region of the temples and top of the head.

We shall find that a proper level of emotions accompany a person's thoughts if the temples show a harmonious form. This is true of temples that turn off from the forehead in front, moving in a gentle curve along a plane that is more or less at right angles towards the back (Fig. 56, over). The two temples ought not to be too close to one another either, which can of course easily be the case when the forehead is narrow; this can also often occur when the back of the head is narrow and somewhat squeezed together (Fig. 57). If we wanted to speak in more general terms about the dangers people can be exposed to purely on the grounds of their bodily organization, if their temples are too close together, and possibly also bend back from the forehead very sharply, we would have to say the following: they could develop into people with very arid thoughts, and they may possibly choose to work in the sphere of bureaucracy. Their thought processes will proceed in the manner in which the novelist Doderer in *Die erleuchteten Fenster* ('The Illuminated Windows') turns his hero's thought

Fig. 56

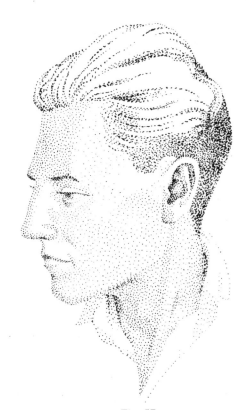

Fig. 57

processes into that of a satyr. They are totally arid and governed by the pettifogging style characteristic of official decrees.

Such a tendency will possibly coincide with slightly flattened temples, even if this is a bit of an exaggeration. Similar forms can also crop up in people whose thoughts are habitually inhibited by a certain heaviness. It is as though the weight of the earth were taking hold of thought life and robbing it of its natural ability to take wing. This condition can often occur in melancholics, and is frequently physiognomically exemplified in the area of the temples and the top of the head in the way we have mentioned.

The opposite of this narrow build is widely expanded temples, and we can meet with every stage of this. This is found when people allow their thinking to be overpowered to too great an extent by the rising up of feelings. There is no brake, as there is with melancholics, no instrument of restraint that can be put under the wheels of the vehicle of thought that is speeding out of control; all perception, mental imagery and thinking is on the contrary caught up too quickly in the pull of feelings and, in some instances, threatens to overwhelm. This can soon become hate or love, courage or cowardice. Where some cholerics are concerned, such a formation is typical. The artist Adolf Menzel, who possessed a lot of the traits of a choleric in his bodily structure, also had temples that were somewhat too wide. This is seen in two self-portraits he made. The one painted in 1882 is in the Berlin national gallery (Fig. 58, over) and the portrait of 1837, done when he was young, possibly shows this even more clearly, although the choleric element is much more in evidence in his face in the later portraits.

Imaginative phlegmatics with large heads frequently also have widely projecting temples. These people allow their inner calm, their wallowing in the constant babbling flow of feeling to flow far too strongly into their thought processes.

We still have to give special mention to the back of the head, which is the third section of the skull we have to consider with regard to the expression of the power of thinking. This section reveals how intensely the life of thoughts is accompanied by the will. It is a quite special ability of human beings that, arising out of a mental image, a thought they have grasped, they are able to *do* something. The action

Fig. 58

of an animal, arising as it does out of a sense impression, takes place as an unconscious reflex. However, the more that human beings master their thinking the more they will sense that every act of real thinking and reflecting includes a strong element of will force. This is just an indication; Rudolf Steiner in one of his most important fundamental books, *The Philosophy of Freedom,* gives more details in a thoroughly philosophical way. It is a matter of the strength of a personality how strongly they sense the will hidden in their thinking. This means, however, that they can perform their actions in the full consciousness of their thinking. If they succeed in this then this takes place with full freedom of the will. The spiritual strength of the personality is seen at its most visible in well-considered action, in the real engagement of the free will.

The most important thing for our physiognomical study is to discover where the will that is constantly working into the head organization actually manifests. Generally speaking the chief area is the back of the head. Even if this has to be taken with a grain of salt, it can certainly be said that we have to distinguish two opposites. On the one hand there are the people with a well-shaped curve at the back of their heads. We can usually register a forceful will element in their thought life; they are liberated people who want to have the freedom to develop themselves. Also spiritually refined individuals, who have at least the possibility of working on themselves, possess the kind of back to their heads shaped as we have described (Fig. 59).

On the other hand there is the kind of form where the curve at the

Fig. 59

Fig. 60

back of the head is too short, its appearance flat, so that it runs on, interrupting the straight line running towards the neck. At the same time we will often encounter a kind of bull neck. This poor development of the back of the head is usually an expression of a person with a will largely directed to the material world. The spiritual dimension has not prepared itself a space in which the will can be mirrored in a finer form. Therefore we shall not be astonished to find a formation such as this linked with a certain coarseness, even brutality of character (Fig. 60).

★

Having dealt with more general aspects of the form of the skull we will now look at particular examples of the forehead. It is fundamentally a dominant part of the face, and therefore plays a very important role in our whole expression. As in this area the skin is to a certain extent closely attached to the bones, the two directions in which the forming forces take effect on the forehead are seen extremely clearly. One of them goes horizontally along the lower part of the brow from the side where the temples are, towards the front. This causes a damming up to happen above the eye cavities, whose upper edge forms the boundary of the lower part of the forehead. All this belongs to the horizontal forces. About a third of the forehead seems to be formed by this. Above this are the remaining two thirds, which are formed by the upward thrusting forces, i.e., from below upwards. The forming of the lower part is strongly influenced by the upper boundaries of the eye cavities. The significance of this can almost be taken symbolically, for it shows that, so to speak, the lower end of the brow is being influenced by formative forces that have to function very near to the enclosure, the bone enclosure of the eyes. Now the eyes are among the most prominent of our sense organs, and their activity of perceiving is a very important part of the work of our senses altogether. And so as far as our thinking is concerned too, everything that has to do with what is perceptible, i.e., what is of an earthly nature, comes to expression in the lower part of the forehead. The way we see the world through our sense organs and form our thinking from this perception is manifested in the region of the brow lying directly above the eye cavities.

The other part of the forehead curves upwards and runs on beyond the hairline gradually to the highest point of the skull. This part is to a certain extent released from gravity and approaches the form of a sphere. It is repeating the form of the cosmos. We indicated before that the form of the brain actually brings about the form of the skull. We arrive at this both from our anatomical studies and from the history of evolution. Once we have grasped the cosmological formation of the head this fact can connect up so beautifully with the remark of Rudolf Steiner's that the forms and convolutions of the brain can be regarded as a star-studded sky. Into it stream influences from the stars.[7] So it is no wonder that the brain's bony sheath copies the cosmic form of the heavens! What is stamped onto the upper part of the brow is on the one hand the expansiveness of mental imagery and on the other hand the kind of thinking that becomes free of the physical. We bring the potential for this out of our past—as also in the case of the ears. What we make of it, however, and in what form we make use of it, depends on our present activity and practice.

★

In early childhood there are a great many examples of the forehead being more prominent than later on in life (Fig. 61). This is partly to do with the fact that at birth the skull is a long way from attaining the

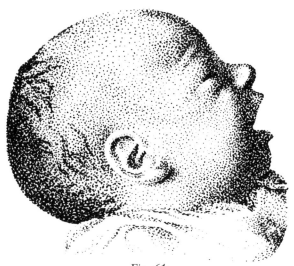

Fig. 61

closed form it acquires later. The so-called fontanels are still open, the forehead fontanel the widest of all. This fact enables the bones to grow to suit the size of the brain and the amount of fluid that surrounds it. The more fluid there is in the brain and its surrounding sheath the more leeway there is of course for a slight forward extension of the bones that are not firmly joined together. This is why the curve of the brow appears stronger or weaker.

Within certain limits the following can be said: an organ such as the brain, in which at the beginning of life the fluid element works very strongly, is revealing in this way its inner plasticity. This is of course of far greater importance at the beginning of life than it would be one, two or even three years later. This gives direct evidence that the high, prominent forehead is indicating that its bearer has had a long time in which to develop the brain. It stayed flexible for longer, youthful life forces at work on the upbuilding process were engaged there for longer, so to speak, than would have been the case in a less watery brain. Therefore a person with a less prominent, a less strongly curved forehead will reveal to us that their brain was less humid, drier than at an earlier time. The forming force lives primarily in the watery element; this means, however, that even if this is invisible to the naked eye, the picture of the developing organ has to be there potentially. The less such a process of growth is speeded up—again, within certain limits—the better chance there is for the spiritual image of the brain, which lives in the brain fluid, to develop its real nature. The consequences will be that an organ such as this, mirrored in the beautiful curve and height of the brow, will have the chance to become the instrument for a particular kind of thinking, namely, the kind in which will live the ability to be active, too, in an imaginative way as distinct from merely intellectually. What has been born as form in so intense a way out of the fluid element reappears as it were as the capacity for imaginative thinking. Special emphasis is put on the fact that this only applies to a certain extent, however. Because if the limit is exceeded, meaning that too much fluid is there, then a quite specific condition arises. The child becomes totally caught up in the forces inherent in water to become round (this is seen in the tendency water has to form drops).

In growing children, however, there is no possibility of their applying their individual being to influence earthly substances. You could also say that they lose the necessary skill to enter properly into their organs. And what happens in these extreme cases? The child gets too large a head, which can eventually degenerate into a case of so-called hydrocephalus. This happens for various not easily recognized reasons, but it comes about easily, especially in the case of a rickety-type illness. With this illness the organism, especially the brain, has more humidity than a healthy person has. This finally amounts to too high a forehead and too strongly pronounced protuberances that are the result of rickets, the traces of which remain for the rest of life (Figs 62 and 63). In severe cases of this affliction the closing of the fontanels is delayed. These children are slow in their emotional responses not only whilst the illness lasts, but even later on as adults; they will be

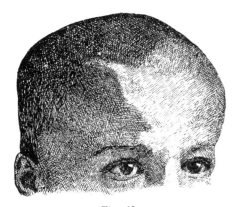

Fig. 62

Fig. 63

lumbering and phlegmatic both in their behaviour and their thinking. We shall also find that the form of their forehead becomes coarser in these cases. Even in later years it is possible to see that in the earliest years of a child that had rickets the structural forces, with their power of plasticity, did not have that very fine ability to mould and form that is normally there in a healthy child.

Something else too, can be read from a phenomenon such as this. At certain particular times in life, the formative force reaches a particular strength in certain organs, which it never attains again. If the modelling of the forehead cannot be carried out with maximum precision by the particular moment when the fontanels would close in the case of a healthy child, then the proper formative force will not penetrate the bones later on in full strength. A similar situation occurs in the case of a bone fracture and also following most injuries to the body. Structural activity certainly takes place in full force at the spot where the break was, or the wound, but usually total success is not achieved in the restoration of the form. We are left with small unevennesses or larger, thickened scars.

★

There belongs to this study of the two parts of the forehead the remarkable phenomenon from a previous cultural epoch in which people apparently only attached significance to the upper parts of it. This appears to have been especially the case in the time of ancient Greece. In ideal portrayals of gods and also of some figures of heroes in Greek art, we come across brows that go straight up without any diversion. We see this upward-reaching force emphasized in the way the bridge of the nose passes without interruption into the forehead. In addition to this, in examples of both gods and many of the heroes, the principle of the curve is expressed also in the enormous helmet. This is almost a regular occurrence in the statues of Pallas Athene. She is the personification of wisdom, the thought force of the Greeks in visible form. She was inspired from the cosmos, for which we may also take the helmet to be a kind of image. In that classical period the same kind of thought life still existed in great pictures as has been preserved in Greek myths. The development of abstract thinking in a strictly mathematical form was preserved for a later date. We come then to an understanding of the noble brow seen in the ancient works of art of the Greek sculptors (Fig. 64). We get the overall impression that the actual curve, that is, the imitation of the vault of heaven, is not so much set into the forehead as set into the structure of the helmet that towers above it.

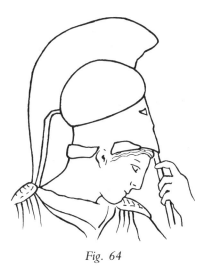

Fig. 64

We can also take this as a sign that the force of divine thought has not yet fully incarnated, but still partly hovers over the figure. For it was in the Greek age that the human head began to become the vessel for thought. This line of development was only fully completed with the entry of the Earth Spirit into the earth itself, namely, of the descent of the Christ. Human beings only became conscious of this at a later time, and this comes to expression in the great painters. This is why we see the emergence of countless pictures of the Madonna. The Madonna is then painted with greater and greater beauty. She becomes the holy vessel of the divine force of life. This is mirrored in a wonderful way (which has special significance in our context) in the clear and curved foreheads of the Madonnas (Fig. 65, over). They are intended to portray the heavenly force of thinking. Mary actually says to the angel of the Annunciation: 'Behold the handmaid of the Lord; be it unto me according to thy word.'[8] And the chief characteristic of the life of Mary was that she did not allow any earthly matters to disturb her, but constantly obeyed the call of heaven.

Fig. 65

Where the 'Spirit of Negation' is concerned it is quite a different matter, for he endeavours to ensnare everything and get it deeply entangled in earthly matters: he paralyses life on earth and draws it away from spiritual involvement. Goethe worked a great deal of this into his Mephistopheles; Rudolf Steiner, however, pronounced him clearly to be the being Ahriman. Whenever there is the endeavour to make this dark power visible in art it is portrayed as having a countenance with a particular characteristic forehead: it recedes in a backward-fleeing movement. Only the lower part of the forehead is given attention and the 'starry' curve is completely missing. We can very often detect something similar when an artist attempts to portray the evil in a person. The small sketch of Judas in Leonardo's *Last Supper* is worth a mention.

★

For the people of the present time it would be desirable if both kinds of thought formation were to be held in balance. This only comes about when adults reach maturity, although it is being prepared for in the preceding years. We must bear in mind here that thinking in pictures, all forms of grasping the world pictorially, belongs more to children before the age of puberty, whilst the possibility of thinking in mathematical, conceptual form only develops later. To what extent all this is being prepared for in the child's earlier years becomes manifest in the two parts of the forehead after the closing up of the large fontanel, which in the case of a normal healthy child is in the second year.

In general we can also say that there is the tendency in females to develop the upper part of the forehead more strongly and the lower half less strongly. By and large this is less the case in males. The reason for this is the fact that in women imaginative thinking predominates compared to the logical, mathematical thinking of a man. All this relates primarily to the basic structure which has been in the process of preparation, and which can be read in the face. Here, too, it has to be left open to what extent children develop these potential possibilities further in their early years, or let inborn gifts remain unused. However, on the other hand, despite inherent weakness, people can by means of their spiritual strength develop capacities that don't happen to be 'inscribed on their brow'. When undertaking physiognomical investigations one should always keep this in mind, so as to avoid being dogmatic or passing shallow judgement on our fellow human beings.

The stronger development of the lower half of the forehead compared to the upper half points to the fact that the forces of gravity have been working strongly in the organism. If the borderline between the upper and the lower half becomes very obvious, so that the arches above the eyes protrude somewhat forcefully and there is a thickening above them, this usually implies that people are strongly under the influence of gravity. They are either dyed-in-the-wool materialists or their actions are primarily directed to the material plane. They have a tendency to ossify and to harden at an early age (Fig. 66, over). If this becomes even more pronounced it can show a pathological level of stiffening in the soul realm. This is strongly increased if the protuberance in the lower part of the middle of the nose, in the region of the root of the nose, becomes

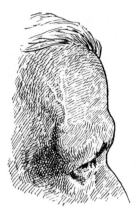

Fig. 66

visible. Of course one should never want to nail down a person's character because of a feature of this kind. But in cases where children lose touch with nature too early, and their life forces ebb, the forms we have mentioned are not at all so rare and point to a risk of getting certain psychological disturbances. The thinking may become brooding, and lead to melancholy or to deep-lying depression. All the symptoms of a dissipation of the soul functions can finally lead to so-called schizophrenia (Fig. 67); for in cases of this illness the soul forces can no longer take hold of the body properly, because it has so to speak become too lifeless and wooden and succumbs too much to gravity.

Fig. 67

★

The two forces that become visible on the brow by the form of the relevant bones can be found and interpreted in everybody. Now it is a very remarkable thing that these forming forces in the forehead area have not only been at work in early childhood and have modelled the bony structure, but we can throughout the whole of life actually still see the effects of this activity busily at work. For example, this is the case as soon as we notice the facial gestures that arise through the mobility of the skin covering the brow. As movement takes place, these forces become externalized and are continually—at least while we are awake—inscribing their runes into our skin. This is how so-called wrinkles arise or, in the present case, the furrows on the brow. Below, in the more earthly part, the wrinkles draw in from the sides and conglomerate above the root of the nose. They form a concentration at this point, causing the creases to draw into a vertical direction. A mild form of this is seen when someone concentrates very intensely; then the skin draws together from the root of the nose upwards. It is in this area that people are very aware of themselves when they really want to grasp something in thought with their ego. It is therefore obvious that people who are used to being fully conscious in their whole personality show signs of this on their brow. An artist who wants to portray himself at the height of his personal development will find a characteristic expression for this in the formation of these furrows on his brow. Rembrandt did this quite as a matter of course, when, at the age of 46 he painted that wonderful self-portrait in which he appears to be standing there in full awareness of his whole personality (Fig. 68, over). The more intensely a person thinks, and above all the more effort he puts into doing this, the deeper these furrows become. It is as though a person were momentarily facing special resistance. In this state he becomes tense, both in mind and in muscle, and this is easiest of all to see in the mobile skin of the brow. This is charmingly expressed by Charles Darwin in his book about the expression of emotions in humans and animals: 'A person can be sunk in deepest thought; yet his eyebrows remain smooth until in the course of his reflection he stumbles upon some form of hindrance or some interruption disturbs him, when a furrowing of the brow passes

Fig. 68

like a shadow across his face.' A significant increase in this furrowing
happens with various emotions. One of these is mentioned by Darwin
in connection with frowning, and this is anger. Anger is also of course
a direct battling against a hindrance. Rudolf Steiner also mentions this,
that 'angry people furrow their brow'.[9] Rembrandt (Fig. 69) and
Michelangelo (Fig. 70) give us excellent examples of this tense and
paralysing force that expresses itself through anger.

Pain can manifest in an expressive intensification for which the head
of the *Laocoön* sculpture (Fig. 71) is an impressive example.

All the soul processes we have mentioned are connected with a

Fig. 69

Fig. 70

feeling that shows an element of heaviness, harshness and torment and is primarily turned towards the earth—if we want to talk of a direction at all. All of this is reflected by the lower part of the forehead; and this enables us to observe certain subtle details of the life of the soul. In fact we can read from this that in those places where the sense process and a certain way of thinking are mirrored (the lower part of the brow) particular feelings every now and again intrude: anger or pain or anxiety. This is not premodelled by the physical structure, however, as for instance by the form of the skull bones, but arises out of the person's feelings of agitation, carried by the pulsing blood into the muscles and skin. We know that anger can make a vein swell up on the forehead and twitch convulsively.

Fig. 71

All this, though, streams up from below, from happenings in the material sphere.

★

The horizontal creases become visible as soon as people forget themselves, or when they simply give themselves up to the thoughts that want to stream in. The area where this manifests is the upper part of the forehead in the same place as pictorial, creative thinking can become visible. The harmony of the wisdom of St Benedict of Memling (Fig. 72) is seen delicately portrayed on his brow in its beautiful dome shape and finely chiselled horizontal creases. Selfless devotion is brought to our notice in his contemplative posture that has nothing tense or stiff about it. This mood of soul is very similar to the ancient spirit of the East. People experiencing old age in the right way ought to be able to live in their later years with more of

Fig. 72

this receptive feeling. If they achieve this, then perhaps horizontal creases will become engraved on their brows to a similar degree, as is portrayed here so attractively in this picture of the ancient Chinese 'God of long life' (Fig. 73, over). In the lecture just refer-red to[10] Rudolf Steiner says: When someone beholds the light of truth he also furrows his brow; this furrowing of the brow, how-ever, is something that expands the self. The furrows aspire to take hold of the whole world with devoted love, and draw it into the self.

This opening of oneself to the world can also become visible in the lines created by the creasing of the brow in examples of feelings of surprise, admiration and reverence. Laughing, too, which dissolves any cramping or heaviness, occasionally causes a diagonal creasing of the forehead.

The well-developed faces of mature people will be able to show a harmonious balance of both forms of creases, and tell us a little about the balance and beauty they have acquired. How foolish to want to

Fig. 73

wish away all these signs our soul has planted in the body, or even to want to hide them with make-up or an operation!

And finally, we want to mention that it often happens, of course, that one area infringes on another. We can see this clearly in the picture of a person who has acquired the exact opposite of poise. The horizontal creases go down a little too far, whilst the vertical ones reach far too high up (Fig. 74).

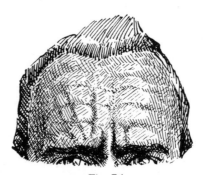

Fig. 74

In old age it can happen that because of the wisdom a person has acquired an image of their life struggles becomes inscribed in the runes on their brow. With a really wise person, however, this can happen in such a manner that despite the vigorous movement of the direction the creases are taking there is a wonderful balance visible between the two forces that are the actual cause of the furrows. Albrecht Dürer's sketch of St Jerome is an example of this (Fig. 75).

Fig. 75

Chapter 5

PHYSIOGNOMY OF THE NOSE AND SURROUNDING AREA

As previously stated, the middle of the face consists primarily of the nose, but also includes the adjacent area of the cheeks covering the same height as the nose. This whole area mirrors a person's rhythmic system and life of feeling. Whilst the head, including the forehead, the top and back of the head already have a specific form which is almost complete by the age of two, the nose requires a much longer time until it appears to have finished developing. This takes place quite naturally during the time in which a child's feeling life becomes more and more consolidated. In *Conception, Birth and Early Childhood*[11] it has been shown clearly that in the early years the life of feeling unfolds only very slowly. To start with, perception and will impulses are very closely connected, and during a very slow process the child's feeling gradually pushes its way in between the upper and lower pole. So it is not at all surprising that the nose does not acquire its real form until the child's life of feeling has become more strongly developed. However, there are always particular moments in the child's development in which one can see the child's nose going through a stronger period of growth. Its form can be observed more clearly at certain times in which the child's personal aspects are becoming more apparent. At these times a further development in the life of feeling occurs naturally. A refinement and expression of the various components of feeling becomes noticeable in the child. It can be of help to make a note of these experiences if you are following up the changes occurring in the further growth of the middle part of the face around the corresponding life phases. At the age of three a little progress can be seen to be happening and again around the seventh year when the child is ready to go to school. Noses often change quite distinctly between the ninth and tenth year. This is a very dramatic time for a child's feeling life. Rudolf Steiner points expressly to this critical stage, and anyone who has to do with children knows exactly how careful one has to be in these years. Children call on all one's love and are extremely sensitive in their emotions. If a severe crisis occurs between the ninth and tenth year it can lead to children becoming deeply upset and depressed, but if properly treated this need never occur in life again. If the opportunity is there, one should look at the stage of development of the noses of a whole class of children of this age and compare them with a class that is a year younger.

The greatest change of all, of course, takes place when the world of feelings breaks through with special force, which happens at puberty. A number of years ago a research scientist, Max Fischer, described this growth of the nose in a very dramatic way. He described how suddenly its 'whole structure' begins, with a tumultuous burst, to grow out of the face of the child in the course of three to six months accompanied by inflammation and swelling of the whole area.[12]

★

Whilst where the forming of the forehead and head section is concerned we are dealing with an area that both from the point of view of development and of acquiring its shape has finished growing by the age of three and is therefore complete, this is not the case at all with the form of the nose. A lot of change will still come about in the course of humanity's further progress, just as we can see that there has already been a great deal of change, merely by looking back as far as the Greek age.

Looking at the ideal Greek nose, as seen in one of the Greek figures (Fig. 10), we can detect a great deal from which we can learn. The direct transition to the forehead has been already mentioned. Let us now concentrate on the particular kind of dynamic that comes to our notice. In the case of the actual Greek nose we become aware of an extraordinarily strong contrast between the upper part and the lower part. This polarity (which still persists today) can be seen clearly. The bridge of the nose draws upwards with the lightness of the light-filled warmth of thought. By means of this lightness it can reach the heavenly vault of the head (the celestial helmet has still to be included in this) in an unbroken line. We shall possibly only understand the significance of this if we allow ourselves to bring a summary of Rudolf Steiner's findings on the matter in a comprehensible way. He pointed out that with the Greeks, thoughts still arose entirely in their hearts and were taken hold of and sensed in that area.[13] A further fact can be added to this, that a delicate stream moves from the human heart to the brain.[14] This delicate warmth of thought streaming upwards from the heart cools down on reaching the head. This was Aristotle's theory which, Rudolf Steiner assures us, survived until the time of Descartes, who speaks of the spirits of life that move up from the heart to the pineal gland. All this is just a sweeping confirmation of what we can almost obtain directly from observation: that for the Greeks there was such a thing as this stream of warmth, and that it originated in the heart. This is one of the directions it depends on: the lightness of warmth, which according to all the laws of physics, goes upwards and consists of buoyancy.

The other direction, however, goes downwards to the tip of the nose, which really points directly to the earth as far as a genuine Greek nose is concerned. (In the case of present-day people a change has occurred which we shall come to speak about.) To start with, through this lower part of the nose things of a totally material nature enter the organism, of course: air, the dampness this contains, and even minute solid particles, such as all kinds of dust floating around in the atmosphere. The latter is of course trapped in the lower part of the organ and sent back out in the secretion of the mucous membranes, or even by sneezing. The damp air will unavoidably find its way into the lungs. So they will be receiving a substance which, compared to the warmth rising up from the heart, appears to be considerably denser and more earthly. This applies already to the in-going stream of the breath, but much more so to the out-going air which, compared to the incoming air, contains not only more dampness but an increased measure of carbon dioxide. So this is where carbon plays a significant role. But this is the actual earthly element, which is expelled when life withdraws. The lungs, then, as organs, are connected the whole time to the element of carbon. They are even capable of increasing the amount of carbon they have in their tissues by gathering in the carbon hovering about in the air as smoke or steam; there is a real force of attraction there.

From all these details there is just one of them we require for our study: the lungs, as an organ, contain much that has to do with the element of weight, with what presses down towards the earth. And this is expressed for instance in the nose—in the lower third of the bridge of the nose, the tip of the nose and in the column of the nose that ends with the upper lip. We find in this region a mirroring of the lungs as an organ, which forms a certain contrast to the heart. The

heart and lungs do of course have a close connection, both belonging
to the one rhythmic system in the human being, yet looked at in
themselves they clearly prove to be polar opposites. Physiognomically
this is of outstanding importance and can probably be seen most easily
when we return to looking at a Greek nose. The bridge of the nose
from top to bottom shows an axis that when the human being (or god)
is standing upright proceeds strictly at right angles to the ground. This
has, however, gradually changed in that the forehead area has developed more strongly, reaching as it were a little way into the middle
organization. (For the time being we are considering only what we
can obtain purely from comparing the outward appearance.) This has
led to the arising of the 'modern' form of nose. Here, the continuation
of the frontal bone (Figs 55 and 56) above the nasal bone (called in
anatomy the pars nasalis ossis frontalis) presses into the nose from
above, causing a buckling or kink. The bridge of the nose, compared
to the set-up of a Greek nose, acquires a wrong direction. The delicate
flow of warmth going upwards from the heart still persists, of course,
but there arises a kind of break at the point where the nose and the
forehead meet. This is actually when the threefold nature of the face
first makes its physical appearance. There is a very important spiritual
background to this dent. It coincides with a kind of psychological
organ of perception, which is of course not physically visible but lies
exactly in the centre between the two eyes.[15] It is also the spot we are
particularly aware of when we concentrate hard, which was mentioned before when discussing the vertical furrows on the brow. It is in
this region that we take hold of ourselves, from the thought aspect, as a
personality. As though unconsciously, some people put three of their
fingers on this spot (thumb, middle finger and index finger) when they
are thinking hard, in an effort to get hold of a particular thought.

This capacity to take hold of oneself as an individual in full consciousness has only gradually become possible in the course of human
evolution. We see an image of this in our own cultural era in the
transformation of the nose in the way we have shown.

★

A point worth noting in a physiognomical study of the nose is the
following physiognomical/anatomical fact. When the inhaled air

gets inside the nose it goes for a short part of its way in a horizontal direction and then it goes downwards into the lungs. This lower section of the nose is also called pars respiratoria (breathing part). The downward direction plays an important role here. Above this is the area where we smell, the pars olfactoria, which is best developed in the upper section of the nose. Of main importance for this area is the upward direction. To be receptive for smell the air has to rise high up into the nose. What we perceive in the way of fragrant substances consists of the most delicate matter we know. The experience of smell itself relates strongly to the heart. The scents we perceive have a delicate influence on the emotions of our heart. The experience of smelling combines strongly—on the soul level— with heart experience to the extent that this is connected with warmth. Therefore a smell can easily influence our feeling. If we wish to express to someone our loving admiration, we give flowers, preferably scented roses.

So also with regard to what the nose does we can see the contrast between the upward striving of substance, so delicate as hardly to be material any more, and the quantity of air constantly being taken down to the lungs, which simply goes straight down. Even though all this is happening in the element of air, we nevertheless see that *lightness*, buoyancy, lives in the one process, whereas in the other the process is much more one of *weight*. There, polar opposites in the rhythmic system itself point simply to the lungs and the heart. Reading the form language of the nose tells us that going upwards it is more the heart element we encounter and going downwards more the lung element.

★

Just as the force in the forehead pushes its way into the nose from above, the influence of the metabolism is visibly active in the nose area, pushing up from below. In fact the form and width of the side of the nose has actually to do with reflecting processes taking place in the digestive system. So we do not mean the tip of the nose or the septum. In the case of infants, where the rhythm only slowly becomes established, the nose is one of the least developed parts of the face, at least as regards its being really representative of the middle organism. But the lowermost part, with its two extended sides, is clearly there. This is simply a mirroring of the fact that in children the process of building up the body plays an important part. (We attach practical significance to this by weighing them frequently in the early part of their lives.) You only have to look at a number of photos of infants and you will be surprised to notice that the area around the opening and the sides of the nose is the only part that stands out. This is seen quite clearly in pictures of both a three-day-old baby (Fig. 76) and one of about ten weeks old (Fig. 5), and is almost unchanged, however, in a two-year-old (Fig. 6); in many instances it can go on like this until the age of seven, but when a child's development is healthy, a baby-nose should not persist for too long. If it does occur, however, this often points to a deep-seated defect, as is the case with the really very retarded boy (in Fig. 77). Only when we look into all the aspects of the nasal form will we get a clear overall picture of which forces are at work, and how we can endeavour to understand them. So allow me to make a brief summary of what we have been able to establish up to now along our path of investigation, so as to help with an understanding of the more specialized forms that are to follow.

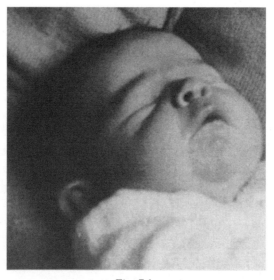

Fig. 76

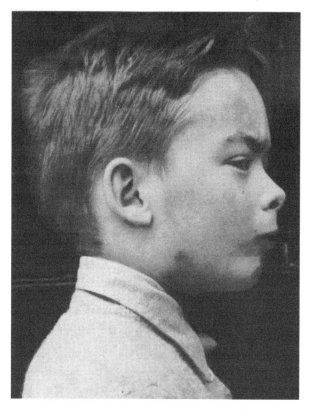

Fig. 77

★

The nose, as a central organ of the face, is a kind of reflection of the rhythmic system. The part that goes up towards the fringe of the brow incorporates more the heart forces and the part going down to the tip of the nose, more the lung forces. The upper end reaches into the area of the forehead and into thinking, the lower end has more to do with the metabolic–limb nature. Physiognomically a nose that has a narrow bridge and sides that are relatively close together and parallel with one another indicates a sensitive heart life, and this can mean a tendency to organic illnesses (Figs 78 and 79, over). Also a 'nervy' person, who moves too fast and is inclined more to the sanguine temperament, often has a nose shaped like this. This form also occurs just as often in patients with too active a thyroid. Such patients are usually hyper-sanguine and most of them complain of having too fast a pulse rate and

Fig. 78

Fig. 79

the heart troubles associated with this. Too short a nose also seems to be an important indicator of the condition of the heart. The significant sign of this is a shortening of the upper section. If the top part of the nose is too small this will, of course, have its effect on the form further down. This makes the upper lip appear too long. The illustrations speak for themselves (Figs 80 and 81). This man with a nose that is clearly too short has suffered for years with a heart defect, a narrowing of the aortic valve (aortic stenosis). If you contemplate facial formations of this sort for long enough, you come upon a certain characteristic in these particular people. They do not necessarily need to be as ill as was the case of the man we quoted; for a complaint that has become an organic condition only emphasizes what may just be

Fig. 80

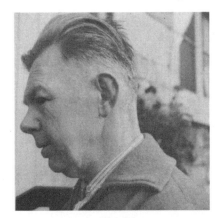
Fig. 81

hidden within. But the particular characteristic of people who have noses that are too short in their upper half is that their bodily nature cannot deal with the warmth and soulfulness living within them. They cannot manage to bring to expression what is actually there in their feeling life and of which they are possibly very unaware. Their organism has become too narrow or has remained too cramped from childhood onwards to fit the extent of their soul life. This condition

Fig. 82

can make someone susceptible to an illness in an organ, which was from the start physically too small.

On the other hand there are noses, too, which are especially long and strongly developed in the 'heart' part. Not infrequently this indicates a depth of soul, which is also capable of coming to expression especially in an artistic way. Just let us take a look at the face of Novalis (Fig. 82) with his long upper nose. It does indeed divulge the powerful force of his romanticism; yet the practiced connoisseur ought easily to be able to predict that this soul is also capable of shaping and expressing the life within it.

We will now take a close look at the lower part of the nose, which is related to the earth forces at work in the lungs, although, of course, the whole nose has to be regarded as one. In people who are harmonious in their rhythmic system there are no such marked differences as there are in people in whom either the element of weight or the element of lightness predominates. This becomes clear when, for instance, we compare a nose with a regular bridge (Figs 78 and 79) with one that has a noticeably widespread tip (Figs 83, 84 and 85). The latter form divulges that the person is strongly under the influence of material forces. The picture we are looking at is of someone who is definitely ill. His lungs have lost the possibility of being able to expand properly. They have themselves succumbed to earthly weight. The fibres have lost their elasticity, and the whole organ is excessively stretched. It

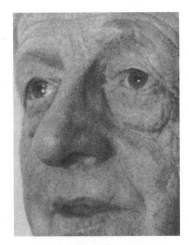

Fig. 83

Fig. 84   Fig. 85

leads to emphysema of the lungs. In the case of many older folks, in whom it is mostly a matter of the elasticity of their lungs diminishing, it can be put down to this sort of expansion of the organ. It is then not uncommon for the tip of the nose to alter considerably, not only with regard to its thickness but also its position. It looks downwards more and more. This is very different from children in whom we usually find upturned tips. In grown-ups the contrast is very striking. A person who has succumbed to earth forces 'squints down' so to speak at the earth with the tip of his nose. Those who are depressed, who feel flat,

Fig. 86   Fig. 87

hard up financially 'let their noses droop' as the Austrians would say. However, those who preserve their childlike lightness, coupled with a certain pert impudence, frequently have a so-called snub nose, with its upturned tip. If someone wants to show that he is, or would like to be, above the 'ordinary' level of other people, he holds his nose in the air and becomes 'snooty'. But which part is it that he holds on high? It is principally the tip of his nose (Figs 86 and 87). This is well known to every actor who has had to personify such a character.

★

There is another aspect, too, that we shall have to follow up, which plays a very important role in the rhythmic system. How does the force working in from the nerve-senses pole find its way in from above, and what is it that makes its way in, from below, reaching up from the metabolic pole? This same question can be asked regarding the life of soul as well, which makes it more comprehensible: how does the realm of perception and thought from the one side and the realm of instinct and will from the other affect the life of feeling? In what way this is present with its individual potential and also changes in the course of life is seen to a certain extent in the form of the nose— one can often tell from this. The thought forces expressed in the forehead have more of a tendency to model straight forms. The nose narrows, and what seems to be particularly important is the way in which the nose looks as though it is modelled from out of the cheeks, which are its foundation. We can observe in principle two phenomena: firstly the forceful way the nose is formed, and the way it grows out of its foundation. This is a sign of the powerful effect of thought life and thinking on human feeling. If we want to learn how to understand the forces at work in the creation of forms, it is essential to remain inwardly mobile, so that we can perpetually as it were re-create the creation itself. This has to be expressly emphasized, otherwise we will merely form rigid thoughts which lead to a dogmatic way of looking at things.

So, regarding the upper part of the nose, we have on the one hand to take into consideration that formative forces are rising up out of the stream of heart warmth, but on the other hand we should not forget that human intelligence also works formatively from above downwards. What we see is a result of the combined effect. Finally there was a reference to the fact that a powerful infiltration of the processes of the senses and thought leads to a powerful modelling of the organs. To come to the second phenomenon we need to mention, however, a weak, sometimes too weak entry of nerve processes, as far as these have to do with the creation of form. This has a very important effect physiognomically, for in cases such as these the modelling force on the face decreases, and faces acquire a shape reminiscent of the ancient Egyptians. The nose lies flatter on the cheeks, stands out from them less clearly. The centre of the face is more reminiscent of childlike forms, which are perfectly justified—in extreme cases—before the ninth year.

Let us now have a look at the influence of those forces which extend into the middle system from the direction of the metabolism, and which have their particular reflection in the face. Here we have to look primarily at the form of the sides of the nose. These usually show us clearly to what extent the metabolism works upwards. If we think again of early childhood, it usually strikes us that the nose, although short and not yet developed much, is conspicuous in its lower part where the nostrils are usually large and round. These wide apertures are caused on the one hand by the already fairly well-developed cartilage at the side of the nose, and on the other hand by the rapid breathing characteristic of infants (Fig. 76). In the early days, in which the life of feeling, though present, is still not yet developed, the instinct to imbibe nourishment constantly sends its reflexes flashing up into the beginning of the child's feeling life. This comes to expression, for example, very noticeably in the signs of contentment and satisfaction in the child that has drunk its fill, and in the pain and discomfort of a hungry infant. In grown-ups the form of the nostrils can tell us a lot about the influence on the soul life of the more instinctive part of the metabolism. In this respect the facial expressions play a bigger part than they do on the rest of the nose. It is not without significance that people say that someone shows us 'friendly nostrils'.

It is a frequent phenomenon to see flaring nostrils when a person is extremely agitated or excited. When in this state people breathe out more than the ordinary amount of breath from their lungs. We get the impression that at such moments more warmth is also streaming out of their nose. This heat is obviously being produced in the places where metabolism is chiefly at work. Primarily it is the liver-gall region that is considerably engaged. If this part of the organism is by nature more actively engaged than other organs, this will then not only become visible by way of the nostrils during an occasional outburst of agitation or rage, but the kind of nose will develop that is characteristic of the choleric temperament. The cartilage in the sides of the nose are strongly rounded and the nostrils open and flaring (Figs 88, 89 and 90). An enhancement of these forms occasionally occurs because the nostrils are open at the side more than usual (Fig. 90). Strongly flaring nostrils develop especially clearly in people with such increased liver and gall activity that it could actually lead to these organs becoming diseased. Certain forms of jaundice and principally the arising of gall stone trouble come into this category (Fig. 91). Apart from the choleric components, the soul sphere will usually show that a strong will force is present in these cases. A good historic example of this is Napoleon, in whom, where the physiognomy of his nose is concerned, almost all the characteristics apply that belong to the choleric temperament. His illnesses affected his gall and his liver. Impulse and passion (and Napoleon was not lacking here) easily convey their heat to the rest of his organism and open his nostrils wide. Old pictures of fire-spewing dragons usually also have flaring nostrils, out of which pour devouring flames.

Whilst in these cases a round form predominates, there is a form occurring that applies to the sides of the lower part of the nose, and

Fig. 88   *Fig. 89*

Fig. 90   *Fig. 91*

which is of a flatter and more rigid shape. This tends to occur more frequently where there is a certain combination of oversensitivity and increased activity in the stomach and the topmost small intestine. The highest increase of this is to be found in some of the patients with stomach and duodenal ulcers. Perhaps from knowledge of pathology we may add the view that among other causes the following can be included: the organs concerned are overactive, and their glands are overworked and out of control. The inner surface of the stomach and the small intestine loses more and more its power of resistance to cope

Fig. 92

with its own juices. So the stomach juice, which contains too much acid, starts attacking the mucous membrane. The ulcers arise through a kind of self-digestion. The patient becomes greedy for nourishment, because this is the only way to keep the overactivity in check. This whole condition often sets its mark on the face in a particular formation of the side of the nose, which is combined as well with a sharp formation of creases at the corner of the mouth (Fig. 93). We should not forget, of course, that people tend right from the start to have a disposition to stomach ulcers also in their particular soul attitude. This attitude could be briefly characterized by saying that on the one hand these people worry far too much, usually about material matters, i.e. money, or their job, in which ambitious aspiration plays a part. On the other hand they also have the wish to keep it all to themselves and 'swallow' it. They allow their psychological worries to plunge too deeply into their physical body. If this penetration is especially in the region of the stomach and the small intestine, then, as we said, ulcers can gradually form at a susceptible spot. A mirror image of the condition actually goes as far as the area of the lower nose.

Fig. 93

A further aspect that is of significance in connection with the shaping of this lower section is the instinctive life that has to do with sex. This becomes clearly visible in extreme cases in which even though the sides of the nose are puffed up to some extent they are different from those of a choleric person. The round shape, which was emphasized in cases of gall trouble, recedes and the mucous membrane surrounding the so-called septum becomes visible. Among primitive peoples, where they still like to display an emphasis on sexual functions, they have a special liking for adding decoration to this part of their noses, as we can see by this ring in the nose of a Native American woman (Fig. 94) or indeed this wooden peg worn by a young Aus-

Fig. 94

tralian (Fig. 95). This particular place that has to be pierced to enable the decoration to be worn is physiologically very remarkable. This is the very spot where there are a great many small blood vessels which often swell up during menstruation; in fact, under special circumstances, a strong haemorrhage can occur here in place of a normal period. This is being mentioned solely to make plain that there are real physical connections between this area of the septum and the processes that take place in the sexual organs.

To anticipate contradictions with the previously-mentioned facts let us bear the following in mind. It was shown that the lower bit

Fig. 95

of the middle part of the nose has to do primarily with the lungs. Finally we were able to mention that the sexual organs send influences right into the rhythmic system. Now it is known generally that the processes in the sexual organs have a strong connection to illnesses in the lung area. In cases of tuberculosis there is often a deterioration shortly before the period is due, the temperature rises, the cough becomes more troublesome, there is congestion, and there can even be bleeding from the lungs. Similarly we often find that the psychological state of the lung patient is frequently susceptible to any emotion connected with increased sexuality. This is actually quite obvious; for the weakness of the lungs in the middle system makes it much easier for things to penetrate from below. This also is taken account of physiognomically in the lowest parts of the nose just mentioned.

★

There is of course also a condition in which the lower forces are weak and penetrate far too little into the area of the middle organism. This is very often expressed in the form of the sides of the nose. We see only a small widening of the sides, which often continue without interruption in the same plane as the neighbouring part of the nose. Formations such as this often appear in faces of the various Greek gods and mythological figures. A typical example is Theseus (Fig. 10). In grown-ups, features like this are often a sign of certain kinds of will weakness. Such people have a constitutional difficulty in taking action. How often we come across people who always 'want to' do something but never get as far as deciding to take the steps they should be taking. All their life long they never get further than wanting to do particular things they see as good or right, but they lack the will-power to carry them into action. Some people show a clear leaning to this soul disposition. These are often just those people who enjoy complaining about everything and tend to look at life more readily on the dark side, yet they themselves are completely incapable of taking remedial action. The sides of their noses have the flat form we described, and the opening of the nose is comparatively narrow—not round but more like a slit (Figs 96 and 97).

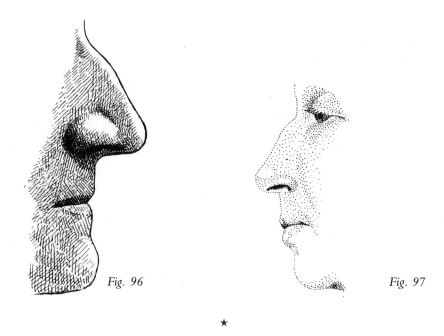

Fig. 96   Fig. 97

★

The cheek area adjoining the sides of the nose belongs for the most part to the middle section of the face. The area concerned has its own special characteristics and it is worth the trouble to look at this in detail. Notice first of all that the sort of forms occurring here are those that can be significantly influenced by facial movements, i.e., when laughing they increase, and when weeping decrease (Figs 98, 99 and 100).

Important in this connection is the difference between a small child's face and that of an adult. With a child there is a certain relationship between the nose, especially the upper part, and the part of the cheeks that concerns us here. In fact it seems that it is mostly the case that infants' cheeks have more of a bulge the more undeveloped their noses are, whereas children's cheeks have a habit of losing their characteristic roundness to the extent the form of the nose assumes a more compact form. We can now raise the question of what this language of forms is telling us. What is being expressed in this development of the human face? Surely these must be secrets of soul life making their appearance in a quite definite way.

In our description of the upper half of the nose we endeavoured to point out clearly how certain thought forces draw upwards from the

Fig. 98

heart towards the head. These thoughts which are infused by warmth, or to put it better, the heart forces that form them, are mirrored in this part of the nose. In the soul, assigned to the middle organism, this whole activity of the forming of thoughts streaming up from the heart manifests as the power of reason, intelligence. Yet this part of our soul also contains quite different forces, namely, forces of perceptive awareness, a person's warm life of feeling. This quality of soul has its image—up to a certain point of course—in the area of the cheeks described above.

Rudolf Steiner called the middle part of the soul that has to do with the whole feeling of life of a human being the rational or the perceptive soul. After the preceding description this will be easier to

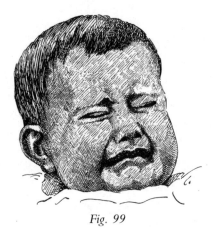

Fig. 99

Fig. 100

understand. A person's inclinations can tend more in the direction of
reason or more towards perceptive feeling according to whether the
feeling, as it rises up from the heart, connects more with the flow of
thoughts in the form of the rational soul or remains more as a perceptive awareness warmed through by feeling, in the form of the
perceptive soul.

So now we will understand more readily why with children, in
whom soul sensitivity is of course only gradually developing, the
more feeling part, the cheek area, tends to play a much more prominent role than the rational part does where the nose is concerned.

Regarding this middle part of the face, it would obviously be the ideal if in grown-ups both aspects could be developed equally strongly. There actually was a period in human history in which harmony did exist in the middle section of the face as though by nature. This was in the Greek era. Especially in portrayals of the gods—which either arose in a previous age or were created under its influence—the harmony between the nose and the cheeks can be greatly admired. This is particularly striking as soon as the head is seen more from the side. The face acquires a look that is delightfully appealing; the most apt word for it is 'charm'. Once you have discovered this you will find it extremely pleasing to hear that Rudolf Steiner said that it belonged among the evolutionary tasks of the Greeks to develop the rational and the perceptive soul. That they in fact did this can still be seen today in the portrayals of their gods and heroes.

Our lives have also been deeply affected by Greek art, and we can see extraordinarily powerful examples of the Greek harmony that existed in the rhythmic system in those times, in a number of well-known pictures. First and foremost let us think of Leonardo with his *Mona Lisa*, his St Anna or his John the Baptist (Figs 101 and 102). They have this Greek charm, and the almost straight Greek nose. To emphasize this perceptive warmth they all have this smile, which conveys spirit and reveals in the face the ancient wisdom hidden behind it.

Fig. 101

Fig. 102

★

Returning to the children of the present day, we again have to point to the fact that as regards the relation of the cheeks to the nose this is another example of the remarkable characteristics of the ninth year. In many cases the preponderance of the cheeks now recedes in favour of the nose and a certain balance is then established. The connection between cheeks and circulation becomes very visible now; the cheeks of healthy little children have the colour of peach blossom which stems from a strong flow of blood in the facial skin. When children are happily excited or eagerly anticipating what is about to happen their cheeks literally glow. We do not merely feel the warmth of their inner joy, we actually see it.

During the course of life the phenomenon of 'rosy cheeks', which every true philanthropist respects and loves as an expression of childlike innocence and joyful participation in the wonders of life, usually disappears more and more. Our age is not unreceptive to this charming sign of childhood. But in a superficial way the female half of (white-skinned) humanity has unjustifiably taken possession of this symbol of childlike joy. Women of all ages are irresistibly drawn to adding a bright red, artificial glow to their faces which in numerous instances lost its colour a long time ago. That they are deceiving both themselves and everyone round them is obvious, but nowadays not too many people are bothered about this. That there were plenty of similar endeavours in this direction in earlier ages is of course well known to the author. But the increase in this habit at the present time is nevertheless very regrettable, particularly because this occurrence also signifies that children are being given visible evidence of an element of deception in just those people whom they love the most and should in fact love—such as their mother and their teachers. Even if this sits deeply unconsciously in the child's soul, this is bound to spoil their love of truth and honesty.

As for the shape of the cheeks, I want to stress a further characteristic phenomenon that is connected with a person's age. Whilst healthy children, when they are not being overfed, have tight, firm cheeks— the most prominent part being in the central part of the face—these lose their fullness and elasticity in the course of time. The cheeks increasingly acquire the tendency to hang down somewhat. Their main focus then tends to lie in the lower part of the face at the side, between the upper and lower jaw. This is a sign of the decrease in life forces. In childhood flabby cheeks like this signify a preponderance of physical processes of metabolism which cannot be brought under control, as often tends to be the case if children are overfed (Fig. 103 a, b). At a later

 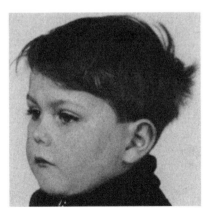

Fig. 103a   *Fig. 103b*

age, when there is often a striking decrease in inner response, the gentle curve of the cheeks frequently disappears, and flabby cheeks come in their place, especially in people who are more obese. This phenomenon is a sign of a heaviness, which accompanies growing older, if people can no longer take hold of their bodily processes so well with their inner forces. Whilst these old peoples' flabby cheeks are developing below, up above, in the neighbourhood of the nose, we see, as a sign of the fading forces of form, the often very numerous appearances of enlarged veins and their tributaries.

Chapter 6

PHYSIOGNOMY OF THE MOUTH AND SURROUNDING AREA

The lower third of the human face, as has been mentioned a number of times, is an image of the metabolic–limb system. At the centre of this part of the face is the mouth, which expresses a great deal of what lights up from the lower organs of the metabolism. Now it should not be forgotten that the processes taking place there are usually totally withdrawn from our full consciousness. The part of them that does repeatedly emerge in our inner life, however, is solely that of urges and instincts. For instance, hunger gives us the experience of a longing, a desire for food, but we do not know from which precise organ the sensation arises. Whether it is the stomach or the liver, the kidneys or the pancreas that sends us the pangs of hunger remains in total obscurity. All that comes into our consciousness is a desire for food. This is the sole domain of the lower organism—the world of desires urges and instincts. The mouth becomes more and more a living symbol of this. Yet at the same time the more the hidden depths of people's instincts open up, they can learn to master them, which is also mirrored in the shape of the mouth. This is seen in its most simple and beautiful form in early childhood. For what does a baby's life primarily consist of? Surely it is the desire for liquid nourishment and the wish to be satisfied. It is obvious that a picture of the instinct becomes visible in the very place where the first step towards its gratification is experienced: in the lips of the mouth through which the milk enters. Straight from birth the child has this reflex to suck; this is one of the few abilities a baby has right from the start. The form of the lips is influenced very strongly in the first days of life by the mouth's sucking movement; in fact it is almost formed by this. By the time the infant has drawn the milk from its mother's breast, both lips often appear fuller, almost swollen. Finally, babies acquire the kind of mouth that is so typical of them, with its open lips that immediately start to suck if anything touches them. A baby's mouth is the very image of a perpetual readiness to suck, which of course vastly increases in strength as soon as there is the sensation of hunger or thirst. It is like an archetypal picture of man's whole instinctive nature. For the aim of most instincts is primarily to acquire something that is just in this moment arousing my desire—and making it my own, holding it tight, sucking it in. Clear examples of this are hunger, thirst and sexual desire, and it is particularly so in the case of many addictions such as drinking, smoking opium and even the ordinary smoking of tobacco. People want to take in greedily certain substances, such as opium or nicotine, in response to their urge to satisfy their organic desire. The fullness of the lips continues for a while beyond the age of infancy, until roughly the teeth have all appeared, i.e., between the ages of two and three. By then a healthy child should also have fully given up the habit of putting everything in its mouth and sucking it. A certain polarity exists between the face that activates the growth of teeth and the impulse to suck, which originates from the lips. The teeth show us an extremely strong power, an urge to shape and form, whereas the drawing in of the various substances by way of the lips leads primarily to a dissolving of substances. Everything becomes softened, liquidized and dissolved.

Among our inner organs there is one in particular of which its activity can be looked at as a sucking in of liquid, and this is our bladder. For a great deal of liquid that we cannot make use of inside us is drawn from the kidneys into the bladder. This is in fact a physiologically active process, as the urine is indeed constantly being drawn out and does not flow into the bladder merely by way of the force of gravity. We owe this perception to Rudolf Steiner, and his knowledge is helpful to us not only from the medical point of view but also from a physiognomical point of view. There is in fact a certain connection between the process of sucking going on in the bladder and the sucking of the lips of an infant. The interesting interaction between the mouth and the bladder is like this: as long as the principle of sucking in through the lips is still continuing, such as whilst the infant is still being breast-fed, there is usually a marked weakness still there in the bladder's activity. The weakness consists in the fact that in the early days the baby is not able to suck for long without soon having to empty its bladder. At the beginning of infancy, then, there is a kind of natural bladder weakness. However, we can make a specific discovery. Whilst most children as early as their first year but at the latest in their third year gain control of their bladder, there are others with whom this does not happen. This is the case with so-called bed-wetters. Among these we have to count the children who often, long after their third year, up to the age of seven, even 14, and even much longer than that, have to pass water unconsciously in their sleep. In a remarkable way their bladder weakness often has its mirror image in the particular formation of the lips. We could speak of two typical shapes. The one kind shows a lip shape which reminds us of the full lips and open mouth of an infant (Fig. 104). The other shape is of too small a mouth, which can still be seen in a somewhat older child or even an adult (Figs 105 and 106). Not infrequently both of these are combined in different variations. If one wants an explanation for such a peculiar phenomenon one could say that in a person who has too small a mouth and a child's swollen lips and suffers from bed-wetting, it is clear that the sucking action in the bladder is underdeveloped

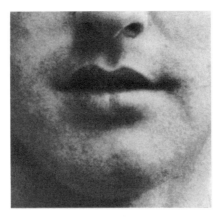

Fig. 104

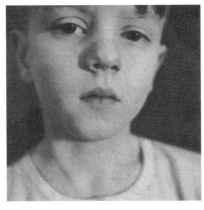

Fig. 105

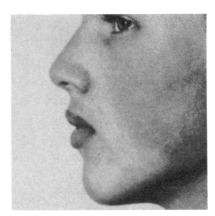

Fig. 106

because it could not be given up in the upper part of the metabolism, namely, the mouth. The babyish nature of the child that still functions almost entirely on the surface of the body must in the course of development withdraw more into the inner region, that of the bladder. That this process has been slowed down often leaves its mark on the mouth area for the rest of life. This bladder weakness is just part of a general weakness of the whole forming of the constitution altogether. People such as this are less capable of building up and maintaining their own form. Therefore the warmth of their whole life of instinct, with its inclination to have a loosening effect, pushes upwards too violently and uncontrollably, and the instincts puff up the lips.

The unconscious urge of such children and adults to dissolve set forms, even to destroy them, occurs not at all infrequently for all to see in people who bite their nails. Those who are addicted to constantly biting their nails, feeling a kind of insurmountable urge rising up in them, are actually trying—totally unconsciously of course—to throw off and dissolve their organism's rigidity and form. So they try their best to bite away with their teeth the hard bony substance of their nails, which is the hardest, most substantial part of them they can reach (their bones being obviously inaccessible). It is no wonder that a lot of children and grown-ups bite their nails at the particular moments when they are excited, tired, or often when they are hungry or actually when they are going to sleep. The condition people are in at

Fig. 107   *Fig. 108*

Fig. 109

Fig. 110

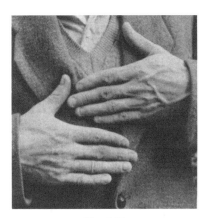

Fig. 111

just such moments is of course the state of being in the process of losing the power to hold onto the part of them that forms and controls the body. So the instincts and urges are free to escape from the lower regions, like the evils from out of Pandora's open box.

Medical observation trains us to notice a frequent combination of bed-wetting, nail-biting and the physiognomical characteristic of too small a mouth and puffed up lips. The 15-year-old boy who combines all these clearly is a good example of this. He has a mouth that is far too childish for his age, and which is clearly too small for his otherwise large face. The lips are fairly thick, especially the lower lip. The youth is not mentally disabled; in fact he is intelligent. Yet he still wets the bed, despite being old enough that he could be training for a job. In addition he bites his nails intensely and with the best will in the world he cannot break the habit (Figs 107 and 108). The much older man (Figs 109, 110 and 111) with the puffed up lips and a rather small mouth has still not stopped biting his nails. He also has a tendency to inflammation of the bladder. The $7\frac{1}{2}$-year-old boy who has a pronounced babyish mouth is a bed-wetter too (Fig. 105). The $10\frac{1}{2}$-year-old girl with the very small mouth suffered until she was eight years old with the same trouble, but has subsequently overcome it (Fig. 112). The other boy, who is almost 11, also has such a small mouth that it would be more suited to a little girl than to him. He has always been a nail-biter, but is now trying with all his strength to overcome the urge (Fig. 113). The 14-year-old also shows too small a mouth, with bloated and slack lips. He is a very heavy bed-wetter (Fig. 114).

In the case of more serious bladder ailments one often not infrequently finds these bloated lips, though a particularly small mouth does not necessarily need to be part of the picture. Characteristic of what is meant here is this example of a younger boy who is suffering from tuberculosis of the bladder (Fig. 104).

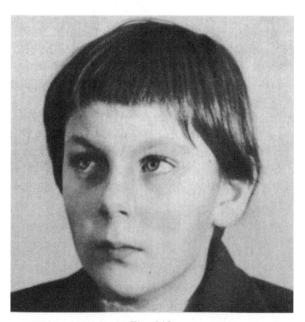

Fig. 112

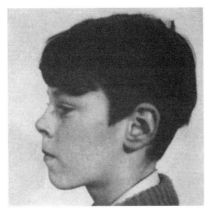

Fig. 113   *Fig. 114*

In many pathological cases all we are seeing is a specially exaggerated form of what we see in a much weaker form in a healthy condition. Where the study of physiognomy is concerned the important thing is that the redness that is clearly there or which is making its appearance in the lips, and the shape of them, present a picture of the strength and weakness of the forces pushing up from the lower organism and the control acquired over them.

★

So far we have been talking solely about increased activity in the life of instinct and how this comes to expression in childhood, and in the course of this we have observed that a mouth with full lips has been a prominent feature. With advancing years, especially by the middle or beyond the middle of life, generally speaking the life of raw instinct begins to recede. If people endeavour to take their inner life in hand they can of course acquire control over what rises up out of their lower organs earlier than this. This too, gradually becomes visible in their lips. Such people are no longer overcome by the instincts that well up in them. Their lips become thinner and sometimes somewhat drawn inwards. This picture of the Doge Leonardo Loredano painted by Giovanni Bellini is a fine example of this (Fig. 115). The mouth shows that the Doge's personality has full control. It is the mature mouth of a man who has become wise in his old age. It is not given to everybody to develop in this way from childhood to old age.

Fig. 115

Perhaps we should put special emphasis on the fact that in the course of such a development there is something absolutely natural about there being a powerful appearance of the life of instinct in human beings in their younger years. In no way do we want to attach epithets such as 'bad' or actually 'immoral' to the various stirrings of instinct which go as far as making their outer appearance. But it also lies in the nature of human beings and the higher tasks, which they are intended to fulfil, that instincts should lose their overpowering mastery once bodily development has come to a conclusion. If this transformation in the course of the life of individuals does not occur, something remains with them which has the effect of a constant hindrance to their spiritual potential. Psychoanalysis and its daughter movements—and nowadays we ought really to speak of its granddaughter movements—have, with a kind of joyful cynicism, placed the world of instinct into the limelight of human existence. And the stage on which the spirit is active remained more or less in the dark. This has its consequences with regard to the way we look at man, and also with regard to a conscious emphasis on certain parts of the face. Hasn't the idea become firmly established nowadays that to stay young means to preserve at all costs your youthful urges on into later years? Though obviously you should also, more than ever, be making the most of them in your youth—for to control and suppress one's life of instinct would lead either to physical or psychological illness. This must after all be at the heart of all schools of psychology arising out of psycho-analysis and its offshoots, even though, with the help of many clever theories, they have attempted to tone down its basic tenet.

Where physiognomy is concerned it is interesting to see that in the course of a few decades the modern world has gone so far as to put special emphasis on the lips, which are a distinct expression of the workings of instinct. This refers of course to the female half of humanity. Women of all ages, with few exceptions, paint their lips to give them special emphasis. In this endeavour, all distinctions of social class have disappeared and, in imitation, little girls often already apply make-up, their mother's lipstick being to hand.

★

If the force of instinct predominates for too long, especially into the more mature years, it becomes a constant drag on the inner life, and many symptoms appear which nowadays are making people anxious and unhappy. Among these are the innumerate phenomena to do with over excitability, states of anxiety and depression. These cases often show full, puffed up lips (Fig. 122).

Obviously it is quite justified to speak in this way about the mouth, but to be more exact we must bear in mind that although the mouth as such is of course a unity it consists nevertheless of two lips. Even if the two of them usually come across as a unity, even when forming facial expressions we can see a distinct difference between them. We can understand this unmistakably if attention is drawn to their different organic connections. The upper lip has more of a tendency to be connected with what is above it, and has a marked relationship to the middle part of the face, primarily the nose. Just the same as with the nose, the upper lip is also divided into a left and right half by a kind of septum that can almost be taken for a skinlike continuation of the nose septum (called in anatomy the filtrum). If the upper lip moves, this always works back on the sides of the nose because of the furrows that run from here down to the corners of the mouth. The upper lip, not only because it is more delicately modelled but also because of its greater flexibility, is daintier, finer. This is why the upper lip appears to be much more engaged than the lower lip when it comes to expressing all the various intermediate stages between a gentle smile and a resounding laugh. Laughter also contains a lighter, more fragile element with overcoming the downward-pulling effect of gravity (Figs 98, 99 and 100). The shape of the upper lip is also always strongly influenced by the formative nature of a person's thought life. This usually applies more to the upper than the lower lip. The fragile, less substantial thought forms of people with a flippant attitude to life is mirrored—if this attitude has become an actual habit—in a narrow mouth, in which the middle of the upper lip shows a marked tendency to be pulled upwards. A thin upward-curving upper lip also marks a habitual increase of flippancy to the point of impudence, when answers are flung out in the blink of an eye. In the course of time some people acquire, as they get older, small furrows running lengthways along the skin of their upper lip reminiscent of the thoughtful furrows on the forehead. They show a certain deepening of thought and concentration. If such furrows form at too early an age, then quite frequently they show an exaggerated turning in on oneself, a reserve that sometimes becomes contrariness, even malice. In this kind of

Fig. 116

Fig. 117

Fig. 118   *Fig. 119*

character too much heaviness tends to make its way into the person and, among other places, becomes visible particularly in the upper lip, which ought to be more of a picture of floating lightness.

A long upper lip, like you see particularly in old men, belongs to old age. Among the various races it is the Native Americans who have the special characteristic of a long upper lip (Figs 116 and 117). In contrast, black Africans show more of a tendency to have shorter upper lips (Figs 118 and 119).

★

The small retarded boy with much too short an upper lip has a personality that is far too light, and is seen especially in his cheerful, friendly nature. Yet his hold on everything is far too volatile, and his upper lip can show this particularly well (Figs 120 and 121, over).

★

Whereas we could see time and time again that the form of the upper lip shows (or at least is capable of showing) an image of form forces, in the case of the lower lip there is a considerable difference. In the first

Fig. 120

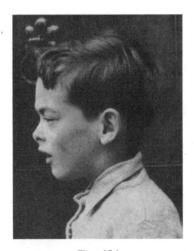

Fig. 121

place it has a simpler construction, with no particular parts. It is plainly a picture of the urges welling up from the lower organism. It has more to do with the element of weight than the upper lip has. Its associations are in a totally different direction than those of the upper lip, i.e., downwards to the lower jaw, which in itself has its own element of weight. As we shall see in greater detail later, it has a relationship to the lower limbs. The more a person is at the mercy of instinctive life the more pronounced is the lower lip (Fig. 122). This is not saying at all

Fig. 122

what type of instincts these are. They can be intemperance, thirst for power or sexual compulsion.

The change that can occur in this lower lip with advancing years is very typical. Whereas in the case of the upper lip we showed that as people get older the upper lip usually becomes thinner and draws inwards more, exactly the opposite picture is seen in the case of the lower lip. In old age it actually often gets thicker and thicker. And when the time has finally come for the fiery urges to die out, then it is not unusual for this organ to puff up in front even more, though it now sags somewhat under the effect of gravity and becomes a drooping, lower lip. Just as the lower limbs lose their buoyancy in old age, the same thing happens to the lower lip, and it becomes too heavy (Fig. 124, page 127). Weight has an effect on the lower lip when people cry, just as lightness affects the upper lip when people laugh (Figs 99 and 100).

As soon as we have grasped the real difference, both in thought and visually between the upper and the lower lip, as we have endeavoured to make clear, there can be a better understanding of the harmonious

Fig. 123

interplay of the two parts of the mouth. It becomes evident, in fact, that the more mature people become the more this polarity between the upper and the lower regions strive for balance. In exactly the same way as we can curb with our superior thinking forces and the mastery of our will the urges that well up and destroy form, there is often a tremendously dramatic battle played out between the upper and the lower lip. What becomes manifest in the movements of facial expressions leads in course of time to the final form.

If this is not understood too pedantically, we could actually speak of two sorts of harmony of the lips, one belonging more to young people and the other more to old age. The former shows a willing acceptance of the instinctive forces making their appearance in the lower lip and at the same time confirming this with a certain indifference, but it is

Fig. 124

mitigated, also, by a kind of charming awareness. The portrait of a young man by Raphael can perhaps illustrate what is meant by this (Fig. 123). The second, latter kind of harmony, the one which it is desirable to have in old age, shows a certain drawing back of the lower lip and an upper lip that has become both thinner and firmer, and which appears to be taking the lead. In this connection let us point once more to the portrait of the Doge Leonardo Loredano (Fig. 115). A comparison of the picture can illustrate for us the ideal course of any individual's development, even if, as in this case, we are not dealing with the same person.

★

Many of the disturbances in the area of soul life or particular characteristics in a person's make-up (having to do with the metabolic-limb system and at the same time even more to do with the life of instinctive urges) come to light in a disturbance of the harmonious interplay that ought to be between the shapes of the upper and lower lips. Attention has already been drawn to the way the upper lip shows signs of particular qualities. The huge divergence that can occur between the two lips is very interesting. For instance, we see not infrequently in older people cases of thinning and drawing in of the upper lip (in other words there is a kind of inflexibility) whilst the lower lip has a strongly protruding curve which can even stick out beyond the upper lip. This is often an expression of an intense desire for some particular thing. It could be that the person has an addiction to money or alcohol, and he makes use of all his cunning to get crafty possession of the object of his greed. Leonardo's drawing (Fig. 124) of an ancient warrior is an outstanding example of the way the lust for power can be so clearly expressed in the lower lip. Also from the physiognomical point of view—as in so many of Leonardo's portrayals of people—this is especially remarkable. It is a very beautiful example of a combination of this aspiration to rule, which is seen in the lower lip, with the pull towards the earth element, which speaks to us so extraordinarily clearly in the lower part of the nose (especially the middle part of the tip). In conclusion, let us mention that a person such as this in whom the lower lip protrudes in this fashion even in middle life will have a flabby, drooping lip by the time he is an old man. This will occur the moment the instincts grow weak and die out; but we can often get a distinct picture of the past from the features of the face.

There is a particular form shown in the lips, which is also not infrequently preceded by facial movements. This applies to a strongly drawn-in lower lip as opposed to a puffed-up one, where this can even be overlapped by an upper lip which is also more drawn-in. In such cases we are concerned with a personality that, even if originally under the influence of instincts rising up from below, has either already suppressed them or is still trying with violent constraint to hold these down from overpowering him from out of his unconscious.

A few further phenomena are worth mentioning. They refer primarily to the angle of the mouth itself when closed. We have to notice whether this is under the influence of gravity to the extent that it is pulled downwards or if it is drawn upwards, which indicates that it is free from this pull, or whether the line between the two lips is straight, showing a good balance between the two streams of force.

A lack of symmetry between the left and right side of the mouth is very remarkable. If this is not due to an illness occurring in the course of life, e.g. paralysis, but is a characteristic feature of the face, then one ought really to give it attention. For a crooked mouth, to use a short expression, very often points to a person who as it were lets his will be influenced from two sides, that is, by truth and by lies, or by egoism and love for one's fellow human beings—in which case the negative side that tends to well up from the realm of instincts usually gains the upper hand. Succumbing to an untruth but at the same time not wanting to be aware of it in one's conscious will produces form forces in the mouth area which normally cause the lips to become crooked. When we come to the physiognomy of the eyes we shall have to deal with so-called squinting. This deviation of the axis of the eyes belongs in the area of the upper part of the organism, and is connected with perception and thinking. We shall speak of this later, but we are just mentioning it here because it might illustrate that a crooked mouth helps us to understand more easily from a psychological point of view that this deviation of the lips can be regarded as a squinting of the will in the lower part of the organism.

★

The life of instincts, which so easily touches and influences our feelings, expresses itself in the lips of the human face. A part of the will sphere is reaching up as it were into the realm of feeling. But also strong, formative forces are active in the mouth area. In the first place, however, these are fully taken up with their physical tasks. These consist in the forming of the teeth. It does indeed require a tremendous amount of strength to give the proper form to such a hard substance as teeth, and to get these to make their way through the gums. Rudolf Steiner explained quite clearly that from the particular moment when the forces that have been working to form the teeth have accomplished their task children can acquire the ability to think, '... and to the same extent to which they acquire teeth, they will learn to think'.[16] This realization is very important for the understanding of our human existence, for psychologically the fact is very clear that as soon as human beings engage their will to act freely they are involving the element of thought. We can even say that when carrying out an action the more people keep their consciousness under the control of thought the more their actions will be free ones. This depends primarily on the connection arising between the area of the face relating to the will and the forming of thought itself. A reason for this based on the theory of cognition, as required by philosophy, will not be given here, of course.[17]

The teeth, which by virtue of their function must definitely be assigned to the metabolic-limb system, contain nevertheless very distinctly a rigorous form-creating capacity. They manifest something of the working of thoughts that reach right into the will. Yet we must on no account want to draw the conclusion that even and 'beautiful' teeth are the expression of a special ability to think. Regular teeth, which are neither too large nor too small, offer no justification for making a judgement about a person's thinking. Strong and well-formed teeth indicate only to a certain extent that the formative forces of thought are able to work satisfactorily into the will. They are often a sign of the fact that the person possesses a certain skill in their hands and feet. This connection between good teeth and agile arms and hands, legs and feet explains why a strong capacity to be upright is one of the things that is mirrored in the teeth; for standing upright is primarily to do with the limbs. The more strongly its force of uprightness is penetrated from above by the power of the human personality, all the easier will it be for a child to raise itself from the horizontal into the vertical. With an illness such as rickets it is just this force which is too weak. The bones of the legs become soft and the child is not healthy enough to stand upright. Simultaneously or a short while later the teeth lose their even form, acquire certain defects, often remaining very small. This can even be the case with the second teeth as well. We could go so far as to say—with a certain reservation, however, for fear of over-generalization—that small teeth of this sort can be an expression of soul qualities, which only in especially acute cases show the symptoms of rickets. In fact such small teeth actually point to a certain clumsiness and slowness in thinking. This relates primarily to the incisors. These show a relation to the force of uprightness. If the incisors show a strong deviation from the vertical direction this points, where children are concerned, almost always to particular difficulties to be found in the character in the way of a lack of uprightness of soul. Upper middle incisors which bend outwards (Figs 125 and 126) sometimes coincide with too narrow and puffed up an upper lip. The kind of thinking that is inclined to be superficial and only too easily leads to irrelevant chatter is typical of such children in their school years. The weakness in uprightness shows itself in them in a lack of seriousness in their thinking, and they usually have such a loose tongue that they blurt out things that are not necessarily true. It is much more dangerous—potentially at least—if the upper incisors turn out a long way in front. They look like shovels, and do not only protrude beyond the lower teeth but sometimes even beyond the lower lip. In people like this the instinctive element penetrates too strongly into the area in which the formative forces should still be the sole forces at work. The life of instinct sucks up the thinking. The upper and the lower incisors characterize a form element of thought that is as though squeezed and forced into the will, and the same applies to the two middle incisors, especially when they point forward in a crooked wedge.

The incisors are being mentioned constantly, as they are the most outstandingly significant features where the facial expression is concerned, and the physiognomical aspect is of course central to our studies. Eye-teeth and molars belong much more to the physiological processes. We can go so far as to indicate that the eye-teeth have a close connection to the middle system. This means that the eye-teeth can be a picture of the way in which the breathing and blood circulation can work into the metabolic organism. A glance at the world of mammals can help us understand this. In some of them the breathing and circulation system is of particular importance. We can think of

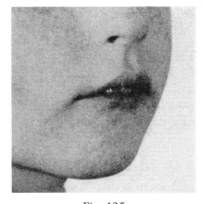

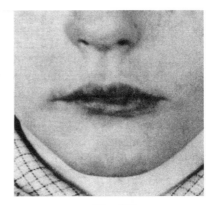

Fig. 125   *Fig. 126*

certain predators such as tigers that appear to be constructed entirely out of the forces of the blood rhythm from which they get, internally, their tremendous suppleness of movement, and externally even the rhythmic pattern of stripes in their fur; whereas with lions, as Rudolf Steiner tells us, the life of breathing is the area of their organism that is most strongly developed. In all these predators, we see evidence of over-developed eye-teeth. We human beings can deduce from these forms how deeply and firmly the rhythmic element is anchored in the lower organs.

People with conspicuous eye-teeth are relatively rare. However, these are very noticeable if the upper ones get too long. This usually gives the impression that the person is not exactly kind or affectionate. There is something far too animal-like about it as is often the case in a human being if one particular aspect of their nature is overdeveloped.

The group of molars, whose significance attaches primarily to their connection to the actual metabolic system, are physiognomically relatively unimportant. They are being mentioned solely because when in old age the grinders fall out this makes a strong difference to the form of the cheeks. This occurrence is of course largely disguised in old age by acquiring dentures. In cases where the particular expression of the face has arisen because of the loss of molars, one thing becomes especially noticeable: as the metabolic forces dwindle the form of the face shrinks too. One way this can happen is that the round, chubby cheeks typical of the years of childhood disappear. Everything gets sucked in from inside because of the gradual diminishing of the toothless mouth cavity. This can be seen in the charcoal drawing by Dürer, in which he portrayed his 63-year-old mother (Fig. 127).

Finally, I would like to draw attention to a remarkable difference in the way the upper and lower teeth fit together. A natural bite consists normally in the upper teeth—the upper incisors—overlapping the lower ones in such a way that with most people there is only a very narrow gap between them. Yet we find repeatedly in children that this space is getting larger. This sometimes happens when the gums are narrow and placed high up. The drawing back of the lower front teeth easily becomes the expression of a more hardened form force, because it is the forces from above which predominate.

However, the opposite can also occur: the lower incisors overlap

Fig. 127

the upper ones. In this case the will element becomes too pre-dominant, as I shall be showing a little later.

With regard to all the troubles that could be mentioned as having to do with the distance between the upper and the lower teeth, I should point out the following: the middle part of the organism, in these cases, has to take a back seat, and this causes an increase in the influence of the instincts. And what effect does this have? The tongue is not kept in the proper place when the child speaks, but easily pushes its way forward and so the child starts lisping. This can sometimes be noticed even without the child speaking if even when the tongue is not active the child lets it protrude a little bit through its teeth. This makes the child look a bit silly, because it gives the impression of a person who is not firmly anchored in the body. This happens quite naturally in the case of babies, corresponding to their age at the time (Fig. 5). At this age the baby does not have any teeth, and has, as we have already made clear, every justification for giving visible expression to its instinctive urges. But later on in life the tongue must stop pushing its way out, especially when children start to speak.

★

So far we have shown that in the lower third of the face, in the area that is the expression of the metabolic-limb system, form forces work that arise from the brain and bring a thought element into the will organism. Before this we were able to describe the way the lips and the mouth became a mirror of a person's predisposition to instinct. In this connection it must not be overlooked that the life of feeling can constantly be swamped from this direction. We have only to think of the years of puberty, during which the world of feeling is influenced tremendously powerfully by a great number of instinctive emotions. And now, as a third element, that is, after the lips and the teeth, we have to look at the particular area in which the will best comes to expression—the upper and lower jaw. The difference between the two of them is to be looked for in the different relationship upper and lower jaws have at any given time to the whole will force. The former points more to the metabolic organism, showing that the will is preparing to be active in the liver, the intestines and all the other organs. We could perhaps say, in a more everyday language, that it is showing us the results of its 'boiling'. The lower jaw, which joins up in front to form the chin, draws our attention more to what a person ultimately *does*. Here the nature of will, in so far as it ends up making use of the limb, makes its appearance in the limb system. This view of the lower jaw coincides with how Goethe viewed it. He described the lower jaw entirely as a limb: 'I look at the lower jawbone as being entirely separate from the skull and belonging among the auxiliary organs. Therefore it is ranked on a par with the arms and legs.'[18]

From the physiognomical point of view, what we described regarding the upper lip applies in general to the upper jaw. With the lower jaw, mobility and its resultant application is significant. It is the expression of a person's conscious will. This is why when a person goes to sleep and consciousness disappears the lower jaw drops. This is something that is particularly noticeable when someone falls asleep in a sitting position, but also on the occasion when—especially in child-hood—our whole being is overcome by surprise, or when we are totally absorbed during a theatre performance. When someone is listening with great interest, the jaw easily slackens, or one opens one's mouth without knowing one has. This happens because with our ego we are outside ourselves, engaged in the play or following the course of a story. But as soon as we become active with our arms or legs the muscles that move the jaw tighten up. The close connection between the limbs and the lower jaw is still visible in the early school years, when the children are writing, drawing or painting. Many of them, and this can sometimes be noticed even longer, move their mouths and jaws quite obviously while doing these things. It is only when writing has entirely become a habit and presents no difficulties that the jaw stops participating in the movement. So we can now fully understand that people who have a strong will and have to have good control of their limbs will not only have strong arms and legs but also a firm, more square-shaped jaw. This is seen very clearly in the faces of mountain dwellers, who have constantly to cope with living and working on hilly ground. They have to have strength in their limbs and this also influences the formation of the lower jaw, which can, as indicated, be reckoned as another limb (Fig. 4). Such a person's will is firmly anchored in his organism, especially in the part of it through which he carries out his will—his arms and hands, legs and feet.

In the case of too strong a development of the limb nature, that is, too strong in comparison to the rest of the organism, the person's chin often protrudes. When the formation of the face is harmonious, it should hardly go beyond a line one can draw from the forehead—nose incision to the incision between the nasal septum and the upper lip. An overemphasis of the chin formation in this sense is usually connected with a broad, angular chin. The bones of the lower jaw then run from the back to the front relatively parallel, and hardly come to a point. All of these forms can be studied amply in many sportsmen, especially wrestlers and boxers, but in outstanding tennis players, too.

This almost always concerns people who, with their limbs, are able to master the earth forces in one way or another. In the days when the task of evolution was to get control of what the earth has to offer, people emphasized these aspirations in external fashion, in that they underlined the power of their chin by as it were lengthening it with the addition of a beard. This is particularly striking among the Babylonians, who had very obvious square-shaped beards (Fig. 128, over). When the hair on the chin starts to grow, this phenomenon, even today, is taken to be a sign that the person has matured from the

Fig. 128

point of view of earthly life. In present times we have almost broken the habit of wearing beards for the purpose of adorning the male face. Perhaps we could understand this from the point of view that by now, at least in the West, human beings have helped themselves in full measure to the earth's treasures! This is documented today even externally by the fact that people's fascination now goes in the direction of dreaming about space ships that will carry them far away to other planets. This remark about the disappearance of beards in the present age should be taken as a thought that would occur only to a person studying physiognomy!

On the basis of this view of chins it will be obvious that in small children this part of the face is developed very little. As long as the child has no control of its limbs it will not show any signs of the form its chin will eventually acquire. This development does not reach its conclusion until after puberty. Whilst a chin that protrudes beyond the line indicated shows an intensification of the will force, even possibly to the point of becoming brutal, we come across too strong a receding chin mostly in the case of weak-willed people. These are the sorts of people who, by nature, have difficulty in actually getting as far as doing what they would like to do.

This has probably covered the three most important elements of the lower part of the face, which have become for us, from the physical point of view, the image of the metabolic-limb system and, from the psychological point of view, the human being's will forces.

Chapter 7

PHYSIOGNOMY OF THE EYES

In the human face the eyes appear as the expression of the personality. In the German language the term for face—*Gesicht*—derives from the verb 'To see'. (And something similar may be seen in the English word 'visage', connected with the verb 'envisage', which is also a kind of seeing.)

We can draw from this, therefore that the most important aspect of the face must have been seen to be the organ with which we see. Consequently they gave to everything that is of interest to us in the facial physiognomy the name 'visage'.[19]

Earlier on in the book we presented a study of the outer ear. In this structure we see a picture of the human being in its entirety, in the way in which the forces of the past of each individual accompany us at birth. The picture the ear presents us with hardly changes during the whole course of our life. With regard to the eyes it is quite different. These tell us directly what state people are in at the very moment we look at them. What they are feeling in their inner being is immediately mirrored in the expression in their eyes. If consciousness is extinguished then the look in the eye becomes empty. If one falls asleep, then the curtains—one's eyelids—close until one wakes up again, which means one is present again in oneself. And when someone dies the eyes are closed, as a sign that the human being is no longer to be found there.

However often we hear Goethe's statement made in the introduction to his blueprint of a theory of colour, 'The eye owes its existence to the light', it may perhaps be permitted to recall it once again as I attempt a physiognomy of the organs of sight. For the most striking thing about the phenomenon of eyes is that they come entirely from the light. And Rudolf Steiner actually adds to Goethe's statement the explanatory remark: 'It is contained in Goethe's world view that Nature creates in man that particular organ enabling Nature to appear at the peak of her development. If it were not for eyes, light could not make its appearance. What is *potentially* there in Nature creates for itself an organ in man so that it can actually be seen by the senses.'[20]

What makes the appearance of the eyes unique is their brightness, which only appears in the light—and is its actual offspring! There is nothing else existing on the surface of the human body that in the very slightest way can be compared to the brightness of the eyes. Therefore a physiognomical interpretation of the eyes requires an understanding of how this brightness arises.

★

An object shines brightly when a light is thrown back from a surface as smooth as a mirror, i.e., by a crystal or a polished stone. This kind of lustre, or one from a finely polished sheet of metal, looks cold and hard. Where eyes are concerned there is the additional fact that the surface is not only absolutely smooth but is also covered by a touch of dampness. This relieves the sharpness of the gleam in the same way as when the light falls onto the surface of water or even only onto tiny drops of water. The effect of the dampness is that the harshness disappears and the light seems to become alive.

The kind of gleam we mean is found predominantly in front of the white of the eye, i.e., primarily in the so-called sclera. But it also belongs of course to the uppermost part of the cornea and the conjunctiva, which line the inside of the eyelids.

A connection to the watery element always points to something belonging to life that is in movement. It is this in particular which gives this lustre its special character, and this is why the best name we can give it is the eyes' living lustre. For if we really observe it, it does indeed give us a real picture of the human life forces. In a more general way this stronger or weaker brilliancy appearing over the white of the sclera can tell us about a person's bodily wellbeing, or one could even say how a person feels in his particular make-up. In the theory of the senses[21] it is primarily the sense of life that possesses the ability to feel its way into the inner situation of the life forces. The first thing it usually senses is the fluctuating nature of the state of health or illness.

★

Even in the case of ordinary tiredness, which makes one sleepy, the eyes cloud over in the area we were talking about. As the gleam decreases there arises a feeling of dryness and slight burning. We imagine we have sand in our eyes. And this is why when children want to rub foreign bodies out of their eyes people in some parts of the world talk to them about the 'sandman' coming to them when it is time to go to sleep. The visible clouding over and the noticeable irritation are connected with the fact that when people grow tired the tear glands secrete less fluid, causing the surface of the eyes to become drier. If the feeling of tiredness becomes chronic we can actually recognize this in the reduced lustre of the eyes, but there will also be a redness due to an inflammation of the conjunctiva. This arises in response to the irritation caused by the dryness. The eyes can now overflow with tears, yet the clouding-over remains because a slight unevenness occurs together with the congestion of the blood vessels. These occurrences in the eyes are very often the result of a general condition in which a person's life forces may be either reduced or even exhausted. We can see something similar happening in cases of malnutrition (either because of a lack of suitable food or because the organism, due to illness, is incapable of regeneration).

In old age a cloudiness and thickening called pinguecula can often occur in the sclera area near the side edge of the cornea. This is for some people a sign that their vital forces are now waning. An even clearer sign is a curve-shaped cloudiness spreading over the upper and lower edge of the cornea, called the arcus senilis. In special cases there is even a slight secretion of lime salts in this tissue, as so often happens in a part of the organism as soon as vitality decreases. Finally, there remains to be mentioned the fact that the prevalence of the metabolic forces can lead to a congestion of the blood in the eyes, which is another cause of cloudiness. This can often be seen in people with a tendency to become obese or to have a stroke, and especially in alcoholics.

★

The lustre of the eyes on their surface gives us information about the body's sparkling life. This is where the delightful and refreshing look in children's eyes comes from, which we see in the morning after they have had a good night's sleep.

However, the lustre of the eyes is also a kind of experience of layers; it still depends on the background that somehow alters and influences the light in some way. Starting from the edge of the cornea, the eye does of course become deeper towards the middle. First of all the colour of the iris behind the moist shimmering cornea becomes visible. The combination of the shine with the iridescence of the iris lying behind it gives the eye the kind of lustre that can best be described as 'ensouled'. For what we see constantly shining out from the region of the iris really is the mood of the soul. What is characteristic of the soul mood is that it is also in constant movement. In a certain sense we may possibly see the seat of a person's mood as being in the heart. But just as the heart remains constantly in movement, this is also the case with our state of feeling; it is constantly vibrating like music does. It is similar with the iris, so long as we are awake. There is always constant movement of the most delicate kind. Just as our mood of soul depends so often on what approaches us on the one hand from outside (such as seeing a landscape or listening to a melody) and on the other hand on the way we give an answer to it from out of ourselves, what our eyes look like depends on the instreaming light and on the way the delicate organ responds to it. This is constantly changing, but only in the most delicate nuances of course.

Even where the most highly developed mammals are concerned, their eyes, especially in the region of the iris, have nothing that is comparable to the expression in the eyes of human beings. For with animals their soul nature has been poured out onto the whole surface of their body and into their ability to move. This is why there is such a rich variety of feathers and fur, and why animals' limbs have such aptitude right from birth that they need no further instruction. Their whole soul has streamed outwards. The situation is quite different with us, for 'so much has gone into the equipping of our inner life, that not much could be spared for its surface.'[22]

The momentary soul state of a person is seen directly in the lustre in the region of the iris. Grief and joy, malice, fidelity, sympathy and hate are all reflected in the iris. The soul element can express itself so well in this organ because its thickness is constantly changing according to whether the delicate iris muscles are extended to a greater or lesser degree and the blood vessels' contractions are stronger or weaker.

★

First of all we can turn our attention to those instances where the gleam of colour arising from the iris intensifies. This occurs when the soul element rises more strongly from deep down inside the person to the surface of the body and remains more loosely connected with this than is usually the case in life. This always happens during feverish illnesses; it is especially noticeable with a sudden fever attack, whereas with temperatures that persist for a long time a cloudiness will easily occur again accompanied by swelling and redness.

People with a tendency to hysteria often have far too bright a brilliancy in their eyes which has to do with the fact that a hysterical person's soul is too loosely seated in the bodily organization, especially in its middle and upper part. These people are therefore continuously exposed to their fluctuating feelings and uncertain thoughts. This whole condition leads to the often uncanny will-o'-the-wisp look in their eyes, which often attracts other people and entices them to find this phenomena particularly beautiful—unless they notice the pathological side of it (Fig. 129).

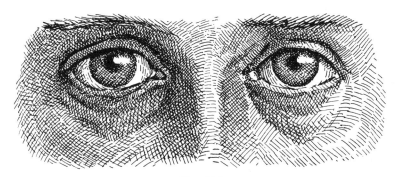

Fig. 129

This fire becomes significantly stronger in people with pulmonary diseases who have seats of destruction in their lungs. In the course of such illnesses the human soul is also squeezed out of the body, remaining only as a flicker. What used to be observed in this respect has changed in present times; we can notice that this exaggerated brilliancy in the eyes of many a patient disappears and even changes to cloudiness as soon as the customary chemotherapy popular in recent years is being applied. We see that it is hardly possible to reproduce this particular kind of lustre that comes from the iris of a lung patient.

The restlessness and fluctuating mood of the patient suffering from too active a thyroid is evident—besides other eye symptoms—also in a characteristic increase in the glow, which occasionally is also transmitted to the skin of the cheeks. (To avoid misunderstanding, let me stress strongly that the skin of course only shows something similar to a glow. Yet the skin of such patients has more of a glow than with healthy people, because it is more delicate, smoother and sometimes even damper.) The cloudiness of the look resulting from a reduced lustre from the region of the iris can even make its appearance in some children. In the case of very small children we can often see this tiredness in the eyes if for some reason the soul element withdraws out of the upper part of their organism. This happens for example as soon as someone tries to get a four- or five-month-old baby up onto its feet. This overtires the little one and dims the eyes. Any overexertion has the same effect; in fact it affects both parts of the eyes, the whites and the coloured part.

We know that with old people the entire light in their eyes decreases, but let us first of all refer primarily to the cloudiness over the iris. This is naturally a much too generalized remark, and applies only to the old age of people who have let themselves be overcome by a sort of soul tiredness. Old people who have remained particularly lively maintain a sparkling glow in their eyes. Soul disturbances, such as melancholy, are often clearly recognizable from the dullness of the gaze. Just as in patients such as these everything comes too much under the influence of earthly heaviness, eyes too can in a certain sense become too heavy, and lose the heavenly spark of which the gleam in the eyes is an image. This can easily be comprehended even intellectually when we bear in mind that the gleam reveals a phenomenon of the light, which in itself is actually something non-earthly, i.e., ethereal. The dullness and heaviness of the gaze, particularly of the iris, is also especially noticeable in some cases of cancer. Also in cases of reduced function of the thyroid, as occurs in so-called myxoedema, or even in some of the cases of imbecility, we almost always see a reduction in the gleam of the eyes.

★

The third kind of gleam coming from the eyes comes from the region of the pupil. This one is the most difficult to describe, yet it can be seen every day if you look for it. Just as we showed before that the ensouled gleam has as its background the iris, which lies deeper than the visible sclera, it can be said of the gleam of the pupil that it has the greatest depth behind it, for the darkness comes from within the eye itself. Through the pupil human beings really look out of their own self. It is from out of the pupil that we really 'meet' a person's gaze. This is saying nothing less than that we are coming in touch with the actual spiritual being of a person, with the individuality. Therefore it is perfectly justified to describe this gleam as *spiritual*.

The great difference between a human being and an animal is expressed clearly and directly in the way an animal or a human being looks at us. If we look into the black part of an animal's eyes the feeling we have most of all is that we are sinking down into an abyss. Otto Weininger in his little book gives an excellent description of what the eyes of a dog tell him. 'A dog's eyes give the irresistible impression that the dog has *lost* something: they convey (as the whole being of a dog does) a certain enigmatic connection to the *past*. What it has lost is the ego, its dignity, its freedom.' We can compare this statement with a human being's situation. In the gleam emanated by the pupil, human eyes divulge that human beings have *gained* something, the spiritual force within them, their free personality, their true I.

In certain special circumstances it can happen that a deep spirituality touches one from out of an animal's eyes, something which as it were is hidden well behind the single animal and comes to expression only in the totality of a group of animals.[23] A rare moment of this kind is described in this poem of an unknown poet.

I looked around the parrot-house
And saw them sitting there with their coloured feathers;
Some were screeching furiously, others were quiet,
Whilst many of them kept flapping their wings.

Some had fetters on their feet,
Others squatted behind narrow bars.
They all yearned for the sun and the air
But there were only crowds of people with their human smell.

The public seemed to stare at them vacantly
Fingering their feathers here and there.
And one of the most daring dandies
Hoisted a gorgeous creature onto his shoulders.

All of a sudden I felt I was being drawn
Towards the parrot with the yellow crown.
The bars of his cage are bent,
And no sound comes forth from its dry throat.

Its dark eyes open wide to me
And my own eyes open up to him.
In that moment both our beings move
Towards those worlds

Where souls flow into one another
Feeling each other's warmth and depth of pain.
O, if we could only sojourn forever,
Filled with love, in this realm of soul!

I am already being hurried away through the crowd,
Still stunned by what my eyes saw.
The small bird watches me get caught up in the throng
So full of longing, left there by itself.

A calm and self-assured gaze from out of the pupil shows the
calmness and self-assuredness of the individual. We can see this very
well when the eyes show a full and rich brilliance; the ego is reaching
out with conscious intent to the object it is observing. If the look is
accompanied solely by thoughts, then it makes a cool and calculated
impression. It can, however, also be full of sympathy and love, and
then it has a warm and kind effect. This is always mirrored in the pupil,
the size of which varies according to whether the iris expands or
contracts. The pupil get larger in the dark or if one is suffering from
pain or shock. That is particularly when a person's ego is as it were

being coaxed out of the body, as for example in certain states of agitation, when people get quite 'beside themselves'. Whereas the pupil gets smaller in a glaring light or when the person is paying rapt attention, as a sign that we are drawing ourselves as an individual back into our body.

In their whole appearance widened pupils give a person a shadowy, dreamy look, whereas narrowed pupils make the gaze look sharp, even pointed. And let us finally add that the changeability of the size of the pupil is a sign of the mobility of the soul/spiritual element. During our young days both of these are rapid, both the change in the pupil and the energy in soul and spirit. In old age all this works more slowly.

So the three forms of the eye's lustre could be presented as a significant phenomenon of the organs of sight: the *enlivened* gleam in the area of the conjunctiva of the sclera (c), the gleaming white; the *ensouled* gleam over the iris (b), the gleam of the respective colour; the *spiritual* brilliance seen in the shine coming from the pupil (a), the gleaming black (Fig. 130).

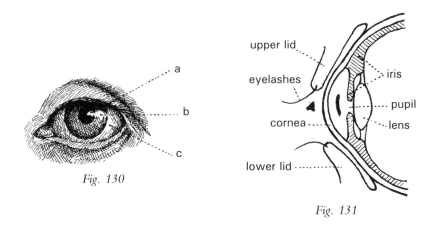

Fig. 130

Fig. 131

The fact is also remarkable that the three areas we have been speaking about are also on three different levels in space. It seems to be the case that in this respect, too, a law is presenting itself visibly: where something of a higher nature is becoming manifest, the part that is on a lower level draws back in its evolution. The sclera, whose gleam presents an image of life, is suddenly transparent in the region of the cornea to make room for the shining of the colour of the iris, the

mirror image of the soul—bearing in mind, however, that the iris lies
further inwards. In the middle this too dissolves, the dark pupil frees
the way for the eye to see, and the gleam that arises here becomes the
language of the human spirit (Fig. 131).

★

Regarding the expression of the gaze it is of paramount importance
that where human beings are concerned the eyes are unmistakably
forward looking. (Despite this the right eye sees a little more of the
right field of vision than the left, of course, and the left more of the left
field of vision.) In the central area both eyes see the same thing and
give as a rule a similar picture. This intersecting of the images of the
two eyes must be given or acquired with the most exact symmetry for
satisfactory spatial vision to be possible, and to avoid double vision. A
correct intersecting of the images from both eyes comes about especially well in humans. It is part of the essential quality of being human
that in other parts of the body, too, this intersecting is clearly pronounced, more than in any animal. This applies above all to the eyes,
and up to a certain point for the ears, too.[24] It is seen clearly in the way
we fold our arms when we are listening intently, and applies, too, in
the way we cross our legs whilst sitting. This action of crossing helps us
to feel ourselves more strongly as a personality.

    If one or both eyes fall out of the line of symmetry, as can happen for

Fig. 132

instance in cases of small disturbances of the muscles which are active in moving the eyeball, then so-called squinting occurs. This has great significance for the expression of the human face. A certain length of time is required in the life of a child until it is capable of looking straight in front of it. Almost every infant squints to begin with. But in the course of a few months this can quickly disappear (although it is different with every child). How capable a very young child is at looking at things shows us up to a point the speed and strength with which its individual powers learn to control the eye organization. The clear and straight gaze of a 12-week-old child (Fig. 132) or of a one-year-old (Figs 133 and 134) can move us deeply because something of the child's own inner being is already speaking to us through it.

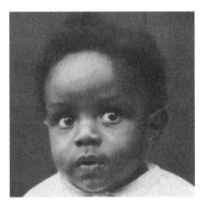

Fig. 133

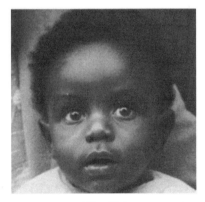

Fig. 134

It is as though the correct state of balance of the muscles of both eyes were being maintained by a higher power, which appears to be related to our own consciousness; for when we get tired, even people whose eyes hardly ever deviate from a state of symmetry are in the habit of squinting. Even a dreamy look, a sign that a person is not making full use of his eyes, easily becomes a squint.

Through the fact that with a person who squints the pictures shown by the retina cannot be quite symmetrical, he does not see the objects exactly where they are. Although the double picture that is then bound to arise can usually be suppressed, the world will nevertheless be seen slightly differently or, we could also say, incorrectly. This leads at the same time to a particular soul condition which seems to attach itself so often to people who squint. They have a certain disposition to falseness. Character-wise they lack any form of refreshing sincerity, and open inner truthfulness as well, and the accompanying necessary love of truth. This applies of course primarily to the kind of squinting that develops early on in life without there being any particular illness that could be held responsible for it. On the other hand, we shall not argue with the fact, of course, that someone can overcome all the weaknesses in his character through his own effort. But we shall find in general that people who squint will easily give evidence of a particular soul attitude of which the crooked gaze is just a visible sign.

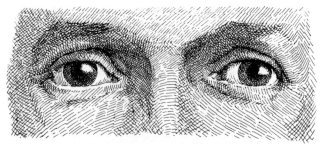

Fig. 135

From the point of view of physiognomy it is important to speak of two different kinds of squinting: firstly, eyes that deviate outwards (Fig. 135), and these often appear coupled with a certain kind of short-sightedness. This kind of squint usually leads to a facial expression that has something apathetic, passive and withdrawn about it. The person is usually too focused on himself, and is only to a small degree receptive to his visible surroundings. The picture he receives through his eyes as it were falls apart, exactly as does his gaze. In himself, such a person can be by nature totally dependable, even pedantically so, but he will neglect the environment. This could possibly lead to disorder in outer life, if the person does not apply all his will-power to overcome his errors. So educating children who have the tendency to squint out-wards will have to be in the direction of getting them used to punctuality, cleanliness, love of order and interest in the realm of impressions. Temperamentally it is more the phlegmatic/melancholic children, and adults too, who possess the characteristics described, and who show evidence of it in their other bodily forms.

An opposite form of squinting, namely, squinting inwards, is often

Fig. 136

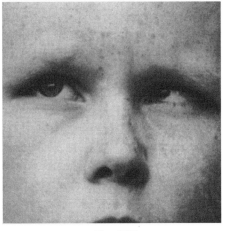

Fig. 137

combined with a certain degree of long-sightedness (Figs 136 and 137). (In this case we do not mean the kind of long-sightedness that gradually develops as we get older, but the sort that occurs early on.) The eyes direct their gaze too far out as it were, want to pack too much into their field of vision, and this makes the axis of sight overlap. The expression is of a kind of greediness to take hold of as many pictures as possible of the outer world. Perhaps somewhat too forceful an expression conveys what is really meant: the eyes' inclination to steal becomes visible and along with it something of the thieving nature of the person. There is a bird that gives us a direct example of this. Just look at the squinting eyes of an owl (Fig. 138).

Fig. 138

This gives us evidence of many of the characteristics described, only in the case of an owl it is just part of its nature. If squinting appears in this form in human beings, however, it definitely points to a certain deviation, showing that the actual spirit could not penetrate properly into the forces of form. This is why anyone observing this has a feeling of lack of trust in the person who squints inwards, for unfortunately he is being shown a tendency to falsehood, to telling a quick lie, to underhandedness, or stabbing spite, corresponding to a look which often has a stab too. Temperamentally we shall more readily find these types among the choleric/sanguines: choler where the eyes reveal a greedy aggressiveness combined with a deceitful craftiness; and sanguinity in the false, untruthful and unstable look of eyes that squint inwards.

★

We can look at the eyebrows and the eyelids with their lashes as an artistic framework behind which the nature of the person appears. These are a very mobile and living framework, especially the eyelids. These close when the personality no longer appears behind them, as in sleep. Then, for an observer, the face loses a great deal of its significance (Fig. 139). In very rare cases a countenance will have the opposite effect, when, even though the lids are open, there are no eyes behind them, as is so often characteristic of statues, especially those of the ancient Greeks. The artists must have been under the impression that in certain substances it was not possible to give a living impression of eyes that shone and were imbued with soul (Figs 140 and 141, over).

Fig. 139

The relation between the senses and the eyelids is remarkable to the extreme. A reacting movement follows not only where the eyes are dazzled, but also when a person is influenced by smell, taste, hearing or the sense of touch. This, however, is usually only the case when the corresponding irritation influences us too strongly.

If our ears are exposed to a scraping violin sound, or a squealing engine wheel, or the loud droning of a propeller, people squeeze their lids together far more quickly than they cover their ears, which would appear far more reasonable a thing to do. The sour taste of a lemon causes a distinct movement of the eyelids, similar to the effects of the stinging smell of ammonia. Violent contact connected with pain also

Fig. 140

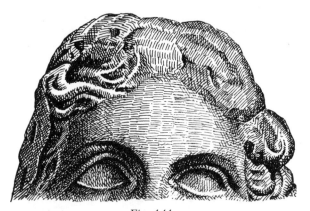

Fig. 141

causes a movement of the eyelids. A significant aspect of all these things seems to be a screwing up of the lids. All this shows us a picture of an immediate contraction occurring also on the soul level. As it is mostly a matter of a distinct narrowing or complete closing of the lids, the eyes will to a certain extent be prevented from looking out properly. Or one could also say the soul withdraws into itself so intensely that it does not want to continue to be open to its environment. It is the eyelids that tell us whether a person is open-minded, and wide open eyes would tell us this—or if he or she wants to brood deeply, which is seen in the drawing together of the lids. A particular character feature can lead to the eyes being squeezed together as a sign of a suppressed soul. If this occurs prematurely so-called crow's feet can be a sign of a person having a strongly hidden nature, but who is constantly on the defensive. All this of course is not referring to many small creases in the eye region that come with advancing years.

Eyelids that become heavy, fat and strongly creased, and behind which the eyes appear to withdraw, express directly what old age can bring about in a person, namely, the feeling that physical/organic complaints do not want to leave any room for the person's real being. As distinct from this, there are smooth, thin-skinned lids that usually open very wide; so these do not themselves appear much in the role of a framework, but make way for the person to have unhindered vision. In morbid, ever-worsening form, this can become increasingly obvious in cases of hysteria (Fig. 129), in tuberculosis patients who show a marked consumptive psyche (Fig. 142), and finally in thyroid patients, if these are showing an increased activity of the organ (thyrotoxicosis). In especially striking cases it leads to very strongly protruding eyeballs (Fig. 143, over). These phenomena we have listed give us occasion to call eyes such as this, i.e. those of hysterical people, big eyes. As a rule eyes differ only very little from one another in size[25]. It depends far more on the condition and form of the lids. Some eyes look small only because they lie more deeply in the eye sockets or the gaps between the lids are narrower. The gaze then not infrequently

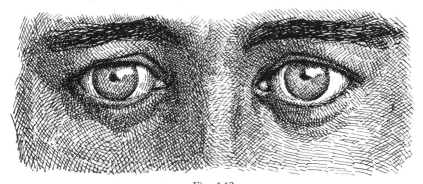

Fig. 142

Fig. 143

acquires sharpness, sometimes even a look of lying in wait (Fig. 144). However, if this form increases in cases of illnesses connected with reduced thyroid activity, then we see all the features that contrast with the increased activity of the thyroid: patients who are slow-moving, are clumsy and usually phlegmatic. Their digestion and circulation are

Fig. 144

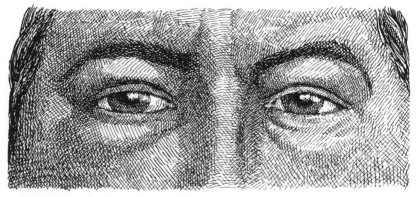

Fig. 145

slow, sluggish even. Accordingly, these people have eyes that look small, and have thick and heavy lids. Due to the various swellings which make their skin look both slimy and dropsical, this illness is called myxoedema (Fig. 145).

★

The mobile 'framework' of the eyes, the lids, are especially emphasized and made visible by the eyelashes. The growth of hair usually occurs where in some form or another a soul element comes to the surface of the organism. Physiognomically, hair can appear as an early indication of the life of sensations. This point of view may be justified by the fact that there are very fine, sensitive nerve fibres in the roots of the hair that bring about a great sensitivity in the hair, and a close connection to the skin's sense of touch. The eyelashes become the delicate watchmen which as it were keep everything away from the eyes which could be coarser than light. The longer and darker the eyelashes the more shadow they cast in the eyes, which gives the eyes a dreamy look. The eyelashes work like the finest kind of curtain for the sensations, and this can also be conveyed to the images we see. If we do not have eyelashes then some of the sensations are also lacking. This is why eyes that lack eyelashes somehow make a more soulless impression than eyes that do have lashes. To be more precise, we should say that eyelashes are the expression of the way sense perception leads over to our becoming aware of a sensation, at which point it gently touches on the sphere of soul feeling. I offer the following as an example. Someone sees a red rose; this, of course, is pure perception. He senses the velvety red and the regular construction of the petals; this is an experience of a sensation. And finally a mood of longing might come about; so his feelings are now affected. This apparently rough analysis is nevertheless a delicate process, and will vary slightly in each individual. And it is precisely this difference that will manifest in the form, the length and the colour of the eyelashes. The cinema culture (or lack of it) has not closed its eyes to the significance of eyelashes, and it produces by means of the eyes of the female film stars, with their artificial and exaggerated long, curled lashes, all the emotions among the audience that they can think of. Heart-rending sentimentality is the foremost one. On the whole what applies is that the longer and curlier the eyelashes are the hazier and more lost in dreams the environment will look, and the shorter and straighter they are the less spoilt and washed out it will appear.

★

Hair also marks off one particular area of the body from another. This applies especially forcibly to the eyebrows. The smooth curve of the forehead, the image of thought formation, finishes at its lower end at the upper arch of the eye cavities. This is where the brows are formed and help to form a division from the middle part of the face. In this respect it is remarkable that there is actually only an upper arch; a lower one would signify an unjustified subdivision—and nature does not tolerate such things!

The eyebrows themselves—not the eyes—signify the dividing line between the forehead area and the middle part of the face that appears below. At the beginning of our presentation we referred to the way the three parts of the face are only gradually separated out in the whole course of humankind's evolution. A repetition of this usually includes recognizing an individual person's evolution. For instance, we normally see, in childhood, the brows as two arches clearly and neatly separated from one another. They leave a free space in the middle so that the way is open from the middle of the forehead down to the nose (Figs 146 and 147). This absolutely corresponds to the fact that in the early years the elements of thinking and feeling very easily infringe on

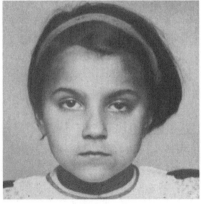 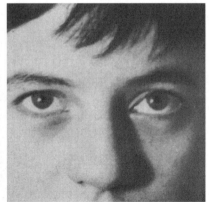

Fig. 146   Fig. 147

Fig. 148

one another. This alters in the course of years, and the same person (Figs 148 and 149) shows in old age a more pronounced formation of the eyebrows, leaving, in the space between them, much less room above, between nose and forehead, than was the case about 30 to 40 years before. This shows a quite natural development. Yet it is not unusual to find in the area above this an excessive spread of the forces that are mirrored in the forehead. The hairline is receding more and more with the advancing years to the point of baldness, especially in men. (Compare Fig. 148 with Fig. 149, which are, as already men-

Fig. 149

tioned, of the same man in his younger and older years.) This shows us, too, the way the thinking forces, which are related to the forces that cause forms to harden, increase more and more in old age.

In this series of brows we have also to include the straight ones which grow very close together as though somewhat drawn towards one another. This very much shortens the distance between the eyebrows and eyelids. When this happens there is usually the appearance of vertical furrows on the brow. The face acquires a worried look, the main reason for this being that it looks as though the eyebrows are pressing the eyes down. The person looks tormented and depressed, appearing to have a surfeit of worries (Fig. 150). An intensification of the tendency for the eyebrows to descend occurs when, as the line reaches the middle, it pushes downwards sharply, as in the portrait of Henry VIII by Holbein (Fig. 151). Underhandedness and spite is shown in this formation, and this is seen at its most marked in the traditional form of the eyebrows of Mephistopheles (Fig. 152).

By comparison a certain openness and willingness to make sacrifices

Fig. 150

Fig. 151

Fig. 152

is visible in this beautiful shaped arch, which forms part of a circle (Fig. 153). Beautiful Madonna pictures usually show these kind of eyebrows. They have a wonderful relationship to the kind of forehead that looks like part of a sphere (Fig. 154).

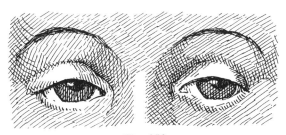

Fig. 153

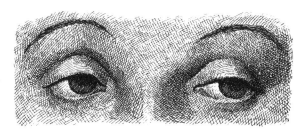

Fig. 154

Appendix

THE PHYSIOGNOMY OF LAUGHING
AND WEEPING

As far as everyday life is concerned it will be worthwhile observing the way laughing and weeping, the waves of pain and joy that move our souls, are mirrored in our faces. We might also discover how much of what we have said about human physiognomy will be proved true.

When we smile and laugh our soul element is released from the body and opens itself to the environment similarly to when we breathe out. Laughing has three stages; these can sometimes occur one after another. But sometimes only the first one need appear, and sometimes the first and second without the appearance of the third.

To start with it is the eyes that laugh. This is accompanied by a brightening coming from the pupils and the iris. This happens very delicately. The sclera, too, shines more brightly, because the inner emotion brings a little more fluid to the eyes. At the same time the edges of the eyelids draw back a little, and little creases appear in the adjacent skin. This smile says nothing more than that the person is conscious of his emotion. He is still sending his thinking into his feeling. Gentle humour is expressed now and then in this form. If someone, perhaps, wants to indicate to a third party the humour of a situation through eye contact, she will give a quick blink with the lid of one eye. With this kind of movement laughter already descends more into the physical—but it is at least still under conscious control.

The next stage is seen in the region of the upper cheeks, where we especially see the forces of feeling, as was described at length in the relevant chapter. The small bulges that arise in the cheeks show the exact moment when laughter takes hold of the feelings. We can see a mother's joy in her child, her love or her loving tenderness expressing itself this way. The rising warmth of the heart is now cherishing what so to speak first appears in the eyes.

In many western countries it is good behaviour not only to say 'Good morning!' when meeting another person, but to smile at them with the middle part of the face: a Central European has a certain aversion to this gesture, seeing it as purely conventional and dishonest. One can, however, understand this action in a different way, for

English people show by smiling—which happens quite unconsciously of course—that when they meet another person they do not want to restrict the meeting merely to eye contact. They want to contribute something from the feeling realm as well, and this is done best by smiling with their cheeks.

The third stage of laughing takes place in the area of the mouth, where anyway laughter usually occurs. The mouth opens—the wider it opens the coarser it will look to an observer—and as it gets broader the corners of the mouth push upwards. The kind of laugh that shakes the diaphragm comes up from the lower organism, and is part of an unconscious drive, coming more from the metabolism. If the metabolism is in good form, as is the case with someone who eats well, then right from the start the person is more inclined to roar with laughter. So we are justified in saying that large people are good laughers—and conversely, that if you laugh you grow bigger! Whatever the truth of this is, it points in any case to the fact that the general opinion is that a good belly laugh works beneficially on the metabolism. When people laugh like this with no inhibitions whatever, they open their mouths very wide and accompany this with a resounding, repetitive ha! ha! ha!

Pain and weeping are also very clearly mirrored in the expression of the face. When pain is felt then the soul element first of all sinks itself more deeply into the body and wants to remain there. This happens by way of breathing in and of holding the breath. So whereas when we laugh and are happy a certain loosening of our consciousness takes place, when we cry there is a kind of squeezing together of the soul element in the body; the word 'depression' means basically just this. Crying begins in the area of the mouth. The lips become thin, they draw inwards and the corners of the mouth drop downwards. The person's will is halted, the processes in his metabolism seize up and grow tense. That would be the first stage of crying.

The next stage leads to the middle organism. It strongly influences the breathing and circulation. On the one hand this becomes noticeable in jerky breathing, and on the other hand in the collapsing of the upper cheek area. There is at the same time the tendency to grow pale, and this can spread over the skin of the whole face. All these phenomena are signs of tension in the rhythmic organism, which can increase to the point of a kind of feeling of pain in the heart region. At this stage of weeping what we see specifically in the face is a kind of flattening of the part that we described as being the particular expression of human feeling.

The third stage manifests finally in the eyes, and this is the moment when we can really speak of crying. The eyes cloud over, the pupils grow wide; tears cover our sight, and people can generally no longer look at anything; the visible world disappears behind a curtain of fluid that streams from the tear glands.

If we examine crying this way, we notice that it also takes place in three stages, which can follow one another in time, as is also the case with laughing. The big difference here is chiefly that it happens in the reverse order. Crying begins in the metabolic system and rises up from the middle organism eventually to the other extreme, that of the senses. When we laugh the eyes become clearer, look out more openly, the circulation is stimulated and the cheeks turn red, the metabolism speeds up and the mouth is wide open. When we cry the mouth closes, the circulation slows down, the face grows pale, and the view of the surroundings becomes blurred (see Figs 98, 99 and 100).

THE PHYSIOGNOMY OF THE EARS
OF TWINS

That all of us possess our own absolutely individually formed ears can probably not be shown in a better way than by looking at the ears of twins. There is often an indisputable similarity, of course, yet this is never so great that there is the possibility of confusing them—which occurs much more easily where the faces are concerned.

A noticeable difference is seen more clearly in cases of non-identical twins than of identical ones; in the latter the mutual similarity is also greater than in the former.

I will start by showing you an example of a pair of identical twins (Figs 155, 156, 157 and 158). At the age when the children were photographed, although there is still a tremendous similarity between the faces of twin R and twin A, there is nevertheless a clear visible difference which, three years previously, was so small as to be virtually non-existent.

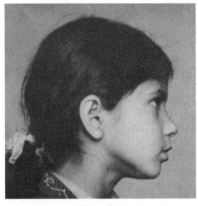
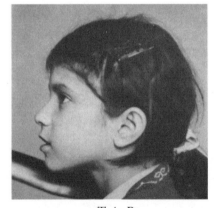

Twin R
Fig. 155

Twin R
Fig. 156

Now let us have a look at the two right ears, from the top to the bottom (Figs 159 and 160). If we refer to Fig. 11 (page 22), at the top end we see on the outside ridge (Fig. 11, a) the following differences: twin R's ear has a more rounded shape than twin A's. This indicates that in her whole being twin A is heavier than twin R. This is also

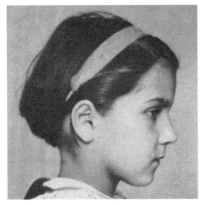

Twin A
Fig. 157

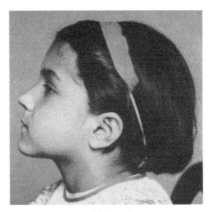

Twin A
Fig. 158

evident from the fact that A puts on fat easily, whereas R is not at all inclined to do this.

The topmost part of R's ear (Fig. 11, b) weighs down more heavily and is broader than A's. Consequently R finds it harder to think than her sister does. The ability for language and an aggressive nature are much stronger in twin A than in twin R. This comes to expression in that the line inside at the top (Fig. 11, c) is much straighter where R's ear is concerned, whereas A's ear has a more rounded form.

The cavity in the middle part of their ears (Fig. 11, 2) is astonishing. Where twin A is concerned this area, though it is not ideal, its middle

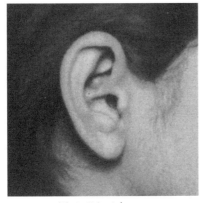

Twin R's right ear
Fig. 159

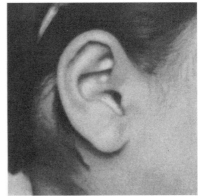

Twin A's right ear
Fig. 160

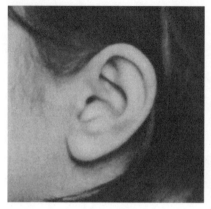 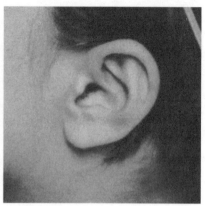

Twin R's left ear   *Twin A's left ear*
Fig. 161   *Fig. 162*

half curves fairly far towards the back. Whereas twin R has at the same place a much narrower inlet. There is certainly a reason for this. R (with the more weakly developed cavity) has had from birth a clearly marked tendency to asthma, which is not the case in twin A.

Finally let us draw attention to the fact that the child with the tendency to heaviness has a much broader ear lobe than R whose lobe, although it is a loose one, is altogether more delicate (see the left ear in Figs 161 and 162).

We hardly need any explanation to see the differences in the non-identical twins C and B (Figs 163, 164, 165 and 166). We immediately

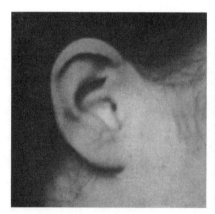 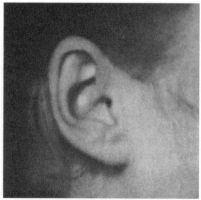

Twin C, right ear   *Twin B, right ear*
Fig. 163   *Fig. 164*

see that the top of twin C's ear has become both flatter and bulkier compared to B's. We are also struck by the outward flattening and the unrolling of the helix (Fig. 11) in the case of twin C, compared to the well-shaped roll of twin B's helix.

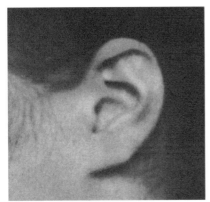 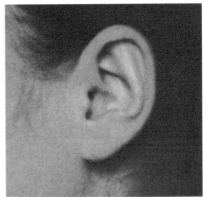

Twin C, left ear
Fig. 165

Twin B, left ear
Fig. 166

Notes

1. In 1917 in the book *Von Seelenrätseln* (*Riddles of the Soul*, Mercury Press 1996) by Rudolf Steiner.
2. Anyone interested can find more about this in Rudolf Steiner's books on education, e.g. *Education of the Child*, Anthroposophic Press 1996.
3. See Rudolf Steiner, *The Riddles of Philosophy*, Vol. I, Anthroposophic Press 1973.
4. A drawing executed according to a fifteenth-century presentation. It shows a Greek influence.
5. Rudolf Steiner went into considerable detail about this for teachers and therapists.
6. See Rudolf Steiner, *Theosophy*, Rudolf Steiner Press 1989.
7. It is not by chance that the genius of language created (in German) the inner connection of sounds between *Stirn* (forehead) and *Gestirn* (stars).
8. Luke 1:38.
9. Rudolf Steiner, 'The Mission of Truth', in *Transforming the Soul*, Vol. 1, Rudolf Steiner Press 2005.
10. Ibid.
11. N. Glas, *Conception, Birth and Early Childhood*, Anthroposophic Press, 1983.
12. Max Fischer, *Archiv für Frauenheilkunde*, 16 March 1930.
13. See the first volume of Rudolf Steiner's *Riddles of Philosophy* op. cit.
14. See Rudolf Steiner, *The Wisdom of Man, of the Soul, and of the Spirit*, Anthroposophic Press 1971.
15. See Rudolf Steiner, *Knowledge of the Higher Worlds*, chapter on 'Some Results of Initiation'.
16. Rudolf Steiner, *A Modern Art of Education*, Rudolf Steiner Press 1981.
17. Anyone wanting a reason will find it described in detail in Rudolf Steiner's book *The Philosophy of Freedom*, Rudolf Steiner Press 1979.
18. Goethe's treatise on the intermediary bones.
19. The expression 'face' is meant to convey something noble. However, if one looks solely at the part of it connected with eating, and wants to draw attention to something common or even coarse, one says in Austrian *das Gefries* and in North German *die Fresse* which sounds like an animal's jaws.
20. Rudolf Steiner, Introduction to Goethe's natural scientific works.

21. See N. Glas, *Gefährdung und Heilung, der Sinne* (The endangering and the healing of the senses), Stuttgart 1958.
22. Goethe, *Entwurf einer Farbenlehre* (Blueprint of a theory of colour), Par. 667.
23. Rudolf Steiner speaks in this regard of an animal group soul, a spiritual being with ego character.
24. See N. Glas, *Gefährdung und Heilung der Sinne* (The endangering and healing of the senses).
25. Many years ago the oculist Senefelder put great emphasis on this (Weekly No. 16, 1930, of the Viennese Clinic).

List of Illustrations

1. Drawing based on a self-portrait of M. von Schwindt, by Thomas Courtney
2. Drawing based on a photograph of Strindberg by Hanna Müller-Fürer
3. Johann Kaspar Lavater (1741-1801), Swiss minister and poet, published *Von der Physiognomonik*, 1772, drawing by Hanna Müller-Fürer
4. Drawing by Hanna Müller-Fürer
5. Photograph taken by the author
6. Photograph taken by the author
7. By Thomas Courtney
8. Photograph taken by the author
9. Copied from Egyptian relief by Thomas Courtney
10. Theseus in the Temple of Zeus in Olympia, by Thomas Courtney
11. By Thomas Courtney
12. By Hanna Müller-Fürer
13. By Thomas Courtney
14. By Thomas Courtney
15. From a presentation of a faun, by Thomas Courtney
16. By Thomas Courtney
17. Photograph taken by the author
18. By Hanna Müller-Fürer
19a. Photograph taken by the author
19b. Photograph taken by the author
20. Photograph taken by the author
21. Photograph taken by the author
22. Photograph taken by the author
23. Photograph taken by the author
24. Photograph taken by the author
25. By Hanna Müller-Fürer
26. By Hanna Müller-Fürer
27. By Hanna Müller-Fürer
28. By Hanna Müller-Fürer
29. By Hanna Müller-Fürer
30. By Hanna Müller-Fürer
31. By Hanna Müller-Fürer
32. Photograph taken by the author
33. Photograph taken by the author

34. Photograph taken by the author
35. Photograph taken by the author
36. Photograph taken by the author
37. Photograph taken by the author
38. By Hanna Müller-Fürer
39. Photograph taken by the author
40. Photograph taken by the author
41. Photograph taken by the author
42. Photograph taken by the author
43. Photograph taken by the author
44. By Hanna Müller-Fürer
45. Photograph taken by the author
46. Photograph taken by the author
47. By Hanna Müller-Fürer
48. By Hanna Müller-Fürer
49. By Hanna Müller-Fürer
50. By Hanna Müller-Fürer
51. Photograph taken by the author
52. Photograph taken by the author
53. By Thomas Courtney
54. By Thomas Courtney
55. By Thomas Courtney
56. Based on a portrait of Goethe 1791, by T.H. Lips, Thomas Courtney
57. By Thomas Courtney
58. Taken from a self-portrait of Adolf Menzel, by Thomas Courtney
59. By Thomas Courtney
60. By Thomas Courtney
61. By Thomas Courtney
62. By Hanna Müller-Fürer
63. By Hanna Müller-Fürer
64. Pallas Athene, by Hanna Müller-Fürer
65. Based on copy of a Madonna by Stefan Lochner, by Hanna Müller-Fürer
66. By Hanna Müller-Fürer
67. By Thomas Courtney
68. Copied from Rembrandt's self-portrait 1652, by Thomas Courtney
69. Copy of a Rembrandt, by Hanna Müller-Fürer
70. Copy of a Michelangelo, by Hanna Müller-Fürer
71. *Laocoön*, by Hanna Müller-Fürer

110. Photograph taken by the author
111. Photograph taken by the author
112. Photograph taken by the author
113. Photograph taken by the author
114. Photograph taken by the author
115. Drawing based on G. Bellini's painting of Doge Leonardo Loredano by Thomas Courtney
116. By Hanna Müller-Fürer
117. By Hanna Müller-Fürer
118. By Hanna Müller-Fürer
119. By Hanna Müller-Fürer
120. Photograph taken by the author
121. Photograph taken by the author
122. Copied from Dürer, by Thomas Courtney
123. Copied from Raphael, by Thomas Courtney
124. Copied from Leonardo, by Thomas Courtney
125. Photograph taken by the author
126. Photograph taken by the author
127. Copied from Dürer, by Thomas Courtney
128. By Hanna Müller-Fürer
129. By Hanna Müller-Fürer
130. By Hanna Müller-Fürer
131. By Hanna Müller-Fürer
132. Photograph taken by the author
133. Photograph taken by the author
134. Photograph taken by the author
135. By Hanna Müller-Fürer
136. By Hanna Müller-Fürer
137. Photograph taken by the author
138. By Hanna Müller-Fürer
139. By Hanna Müller-Fürer
140. Photograph (Demeter)
141. By Hanna Müller-Fürer
142. By Hanna Müller-Fürer
143. By Hanna Müller-Fürer
144. By Hanna Müller-Fürer
145. By Hanna Müller-Fürer
146. Photograph taken by the author
147. Photograph taken by the author